ASCENT®
CENTER FOR TECHNICAL KNOWLEDGE

Creo Parametric 5.0: Working with 3D Annotations & Model-Based Definition

Learning Guide
1st Edition

ASCENT - Center for Technical Knowledge®
Creo Parametric 5.0
Working with 3D Annotations & Model-Based Definition
1st Edition

Prepared and produced by:

ASCENT Center for Technical Knowledge
630 Peter Jefferson Parkway, Suite 175
Charlottesville, VA 22911

866-527-2368
www.ASCENTed.com

Lead Contributor: Scott Hendren

ASCENT - Center for Technical Knowledge is a division of Rand Worldwide, Inc., providing custom developed knowledge products and services for leading engineering software applications. ASCENT is focused on specializing in the creation of education programs that incorporate the best of classroom learning and technology-based training offerings.

We welcome any comments you may have regarding this guide, or any of our products. To contact us please email: feedback@ASCENTed.com.

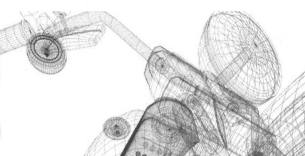

Contents

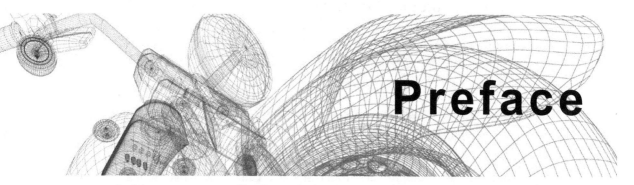

Preface

In this course, you will gain an understanding of the general concepts behind Model-Based Definition (MBD) and why your company is likely moving toward its implementation. You will learn the 3D Annotation tools, which are necessary for using the Creo Parametric software to support Model-Based Definition.

Topics Covered

- Overview of Model-Based Definition
- The Annotation Interface
- Configuration and Detail Options
- Cross Sections
- Using Combination States
- Semantic and Presentation Annotations
- Working with Legacy Datums
- Adding Dimensions
- Adding Geometric Tolerances
- Adding Notes
- Note Libraries
- Adding Symbols

Note on Software Setup

This guide assumes a standard installation of the software using the default preferences during installation. Lectures and practices use the standard software templates and default options for the Content Libraries.

Lead Contributor: Scott Hendren

Scott Hendren has been a trainer and curriculum developer in the PLM industry for over 20 years, with experience on multiple CAD systems, including Pro/ENGINEER, Creo Parametric, and CATIA. Trained in Instructional Design, Scott uses his skills to develop instructor-led and web-based training products.

Scott has held training and development positions with several high profile PLM companies, and has been with the ASCENT team since 2013.

Scott holds a Bachelor of Mechanical Engineering Degree as well as a Bachelor of Science in Mathematics from Dalhousie University, Nova Scotia, Canada.

Scott Hendren has been the Lead Contributor for *Creo Parametric: Working with 3D Annotations & Model-Based Definition* since 2015.

In This Guide

The following highlights the key features of this guide.

Feature	Description
Practice Files	The Practice Files page includes a link to the practice files and instructions on how to download and install them. The practice files are required to complete the practices in this guide.
Chapters	A chapter consists of the following - Learning Objectives, Instructional Content, Practices, and Chapter Review Questions.
	• **Learning Objectives** define the skills you can acquire by learning the content provided in the chapter.
	• **Instructional Content**, which begins right after Learning Objectives, refers to the descriptive and procedural information related to various topics. Each main topic introduces a product feature, discusses various aspects of that feature, and provides step-by-step procedures on how to use that feature. Where relevant, examples, figures, helpful hints, and notes are provided.
	• **Practice** for a topic follows the instructional content. Practices enable you to use the software to perform a hands-on review of a topic. It is required that you download the practice files (using the link found on the Practice Files page) prior to starting the first practice.
	• **Chapter Review Questions**, located close to the end of a chapter, enable you to test your knowledge of the key concepts discussed in the chapter.

Practice Files

To download the practice files for this guide, use the following steps:

1. Type the URL **exactly as shown below** into the address bar of your Internet browser, to access the Course File Download page.

   Note: If you are using the ebook, you do not have to type the URL. Instead, you can access the page simply by clicking the URL below.

   ## https://www.ascented.com/getfile/id/aphantopus

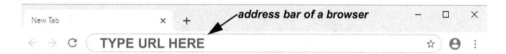

2. On the Course File Download page, click the **DOWNLOAD NOW** button, as shown below, to download the .ZIP file that contains the practice files.

3. Once the download is complete, unzip the file and extract its contents.

   The recommended practice files folder location is:
   C:\Creo Parametric Model Based Definition Practice Files

   Note: It is recommended that you do not change the location of the practice files folder. Doing so may cause errors when completing the practices.

Stay Informed!

To receive information about upcoming events, promotional offers, and complimentary webcasts, visit:

www.ASCENTed.com/updates

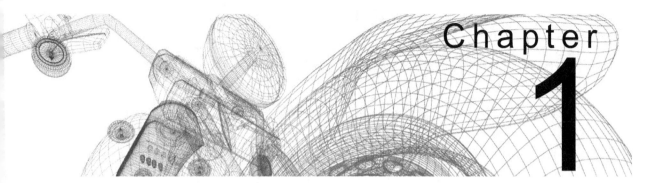

Model-Based Definition Overview

This chapter introduces the concepts surrounding Model-Based Definition (MBD). MBD standards, methods for sharing MBD data, and best practices for using MBD are discussed in detail.

Learning Objectives in This Chapter

- Obtain an overview of Model-Based Definition (MBD).
- Review a list of standards applicable to MBD.
- Understand how MBD information can be shared.
- Review some best practices associated with MBD.

1.1 Introduction

Model-Based Definition (MBD) is the process of storing all geometric, dimensional, and Geometric Dimensioning and Tolerancing (GD&T) information required to design, document, analyze, and manufacture parts and assemblies in the 3D model, thus reducing reliance on 2D drawings.

Figure 1–1 shows a Creo Parametric model annotated with applicable PMI (Product Manufacturing Information).

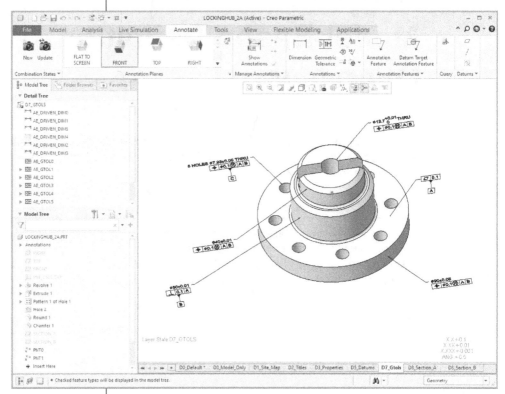

Figure 1–1

1.2 General Overview

Traditional Methodologies

The oldest design and documentation method uses single file 2D drawings to show the part definition and GD&T information. Figure 1–2 shows a drawing containing dimensions and geometric tolerancing information.

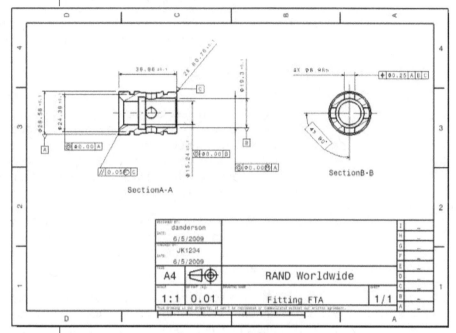

Figure 1–2

Another earlier method, still commonly used today, is the two file system. In this method, the 3D file only contains the model geometry and the 2D file contains the views and GD&T, as shown in Figure 1–3.

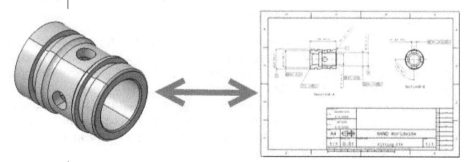

Figure 1–3

Present and Future Methods

Today, MBD is required to reduce the time required to get products on the market without any duplication of effort. It also prevents contradictory information from occurring between the 3D model and the 2D drawing, and it reduces the amount of data that is created, stored, and tracked.

In MBD, one master file (the model) contains all of the geometry, dimensions, and GD&T. The data contained in the model is machine readable for downstream consumption.

- Product and Manufacturing Information (PMI) is easily conveyed and reduces manufacturing costs.
- Quality Control and Part Inspection information is easily relayed.

MBD easily adapts to the First Article Inspection (FAI) process. This is the process of inspecting a manufactured part to the required GD&T data and then producing a documented report for quality control purposes. MBD is not limited to the original Creo Parametric software. Viewers such as Creo View and other third-party viewers can import the MBD data directly into a format that enables it to be displayed.

Within the framework of MBD, you can create fully dimensioned and annotated models, similar to what you would traditionally see in a 2D drawing, or you can create models using Limited Dimensioning.

With Limited Dimensioning, the model is typically not fully dimensioned and a note or other means indicate that the missing dimensional data should be obtained directly from the 3D Solid Model. An example note may read "Obtain values for all undimensioned surfaces by measuring the CAD model" or a similar notation.

When using Limited Dimension models, the accuracy of the model is paramount and careful verification is required before production.

Industries using or adopting MBD include Automotive, Aerospace, Heavy Equipment, Military/Defense, Medical Devices, Electronics, and Consumer Products.

Downstream consumption of MBD provides better collaboration across an entire business model, such as for Engineering/Design, Manufacturing, Quality Control & Inspection, Project Management, Planning, etc. All of these positions can view the data required for performing their jobs. This is commonly referred to as the Model-Based Enterprise (MBE). Some of the groups touched in a MBE are shown in Figure 1–4.

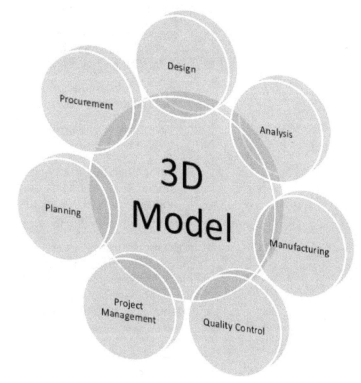

Figure 1–4

Presentation and Semantic PMI

Product and Manufacturing Information (PMI) is presented in two forms. The first form is a strictly graphical form, also referred to as Presentation PMI, which is intended to be human readable for visual inspection and display.

The second is referred to as Semantic PMI, which is machine readable allowing software applications and CNC tools to directly use the data. In this course, you will learn techniques to help ensure that the data contained in your Creo models are semantic.

Basics of Modern PMI

MBD is a one file system and contains the 3D model geometry, GD&T information, and other annotations. In MBD, the model is the primary governing source for documenting your products.

According to ASME Y14.41, annotations include dimensions, tolerances, notes, text, or symbols visible without any manual or external manipulation.

Correctly annotated models provide the following benefits:

- Ensures that the design intent is completely captured, and not subject to ambiguity attributed to non-associative information.

- Reduces manufacturing errors introduced by manual translation of information.

- Increased productivity and quality by documenting the information once and reusing it everywhere.

- Supports concurrent engineering as the design documentation begins earlier in the process so there is no longer a need to wait for the production of drawings to communicate details.

MBD stores the views of the 3D model to display the information more easily. Visual settings are stored with the annotated 3D model. Layers and Combination States are used to control the views and annotations to make the display clear in various orientations, as shown in Figure 1–5.

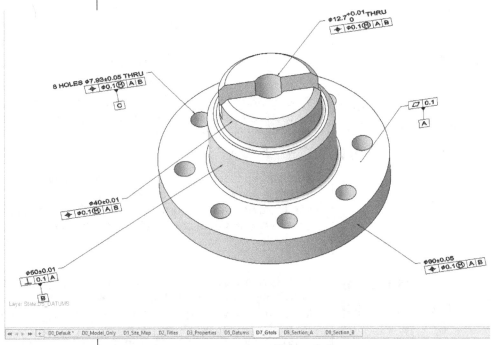

Figure 1–5

Note that MBD offers more than just the way the annotations appear to the human eye. A correctly and completely annotated model will be more easily incorporated into downstream tools and processes.

1.3 MBD Standards

Multiple standards exist to govern MBD. Your company will follow some or all of these standards, depending on how long it has been using MBD. It is recommended to take time and become familiar with them, as they relate to your organization.

3D Product Definition

ASME Y14.41

This standard establishes the requirements for preparing and revising digital product definition data. This standard focuses on the organization and presentation of product definition using the 3D model geometry.

3D Data and Format

ISO 16792

This standard specifies requirements for the preparation, revision, and presentation of digital product definition data. The standard supports two methods of application: model-only and model and drawing in digital format.

ISO 10303

This standard is an ISO standard for the computer-interpretable representation and exchange of product manufacturing information. It is informally known as STEP - Standard for Exchange of Product Model Data.

Technical Data Packages

MIL-STD-3100A

This standard provides requirements for the deliverables associated with a technical data package (TDP).

There are two types of TDP's: **2D TDP** and **3D TDP**. The standard defines what comprises the 2D and 3D Technical Data Packages (TDP). The focus of this content is the tools used to ready your model for a 3D TDP.

At a high level, a TDP consists of the 3D model, 3D PDF, specifications, standards, QA Provisions, packaging details, etc.

To ensure that you are successful with MBD, you must be familiar and comfortable with the above standards, as applied in your organization.

1.4 Sharing MBD Information

Saving a 3D model with all of its MBD data into a single file enables it to be shared more easily:

- **PLM/PDM:** Everyone with access to the model database can see the MBD data using Creo View or a third-party viewer. It can also be opened in Creo Parametric, of course. Permissions on the file prevent the loss of the MBD data by unauthorized users.

- **3D PDF:** Anyone with a Adobe Reader DC or above can access the PDF file created from the model, and review the associated data. The original model is safe from inadvertent changes.

In Creo Parametric, you can save in the native file format or save as a neutral format such as Neutral or STEP. Many third-party viewers on the market can view, interrogate, and markup the annotated model. The inclusion of a neutral format, such as STEP, is typically a requirement when delivering a technical data package to a client.

Note: The native CAD model with semantic PMI is considered to be the Master File. Changes to the design are incorporated by altering this Master File.

Any file created from the Master file (by means of automated or manual translation) is considered a Derivative File.

Depending on your organization's business rules, the Master File and/or a Derivative File may receive an approval indicator (e.g. Drawing Sign-off). A valid approval indicator will deem the file to be authoritative.

You can use Creo Parametric to save a copy of the file as a 3D PDF, which can be opened by anyone with the latest version of Adobe Acrobat, as shown in Figure 1–6.

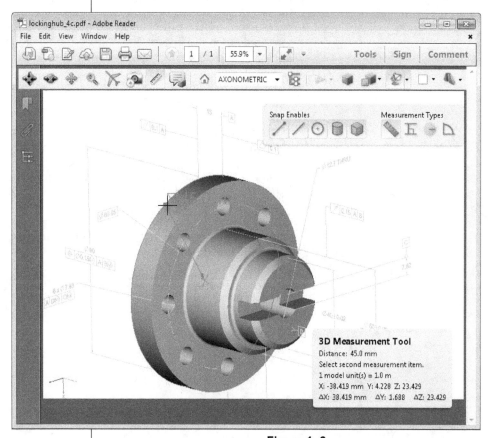

Figure 1–6

Myriad third-party software is available for creating sophisticated technical data packages. This content covers the tools required to annotate your model.

1.5 Best Practices

Some of the recommended practices to follow:

- Develop a MBD instruction sheet (also known as a Schema) that indicates the information that is to be included, where to place it, and how it is to be shown.

- Use the minimum number of views required to show the part details.

- Use combination states to display the part's filtered information and any PMI or Inspection information.

- Name any combination states, saved orientations and layer states that are associated with one another, using the same name so the association is obvious.

- Include only annotations that are required to manufacture, inspect, and/or assemble the parts.

- Follow all MBD related standards as outlined by your organization.

Chapter Review Questions

1. Model-Based Definition is the process of storing all information required to _____ parts and assemblies in the 3D model.

   a. Design

   b. Document

   c. Analyze

   d. Manufacture

   e. All of the Above.

2. In MBD, the _____ is the design authority for the product.

   a. 2D Drawing

   b. 3D Solid Model

   c. PDM Meta Data

   d. 3D PDF

3. There are many third-party viewers on the market that can view, interrogate, and mark up the annotated model.

   a. True

   b. False

4. The best way to ensure MBD data integrity when sharing files in your organization is by _____.

   a. Email

   b. FTP

   c. PDM/PLM

   d. Network drive

5. The standard that provides requirements for the deliverables associated with a technical data package (TDP) is:

   a. ASME Y14.41

   b. MIL-STD-3100A

   c. ISO 10303

   d. None of the above.

Answers: 1.e, 2.b, 3.a, 4.c, 5.b

Creo Parametric Annotation Interface

This chapter explores the Creo Parametric user interface, including the ribbon and the Detail Tree. Combination states and annotation planes are also discussed.

Learning Objectives in This Chapter

- Understand the annotation user interface.
- Review the options found in the *Annotate* tab.
- Understand the difference between individual annotations and annotation features.
- Understand how combination states are used to quickly change the display and orientation of the model.
- Understand the use of annotation planes.
- Understand how the Detail Tree displays annotations.

2.1 Annotation User Interface

The annotation mode is enabled by selecting the *Annotate* tab in the ribbon. An annotated example is shown in Figure 2–1.

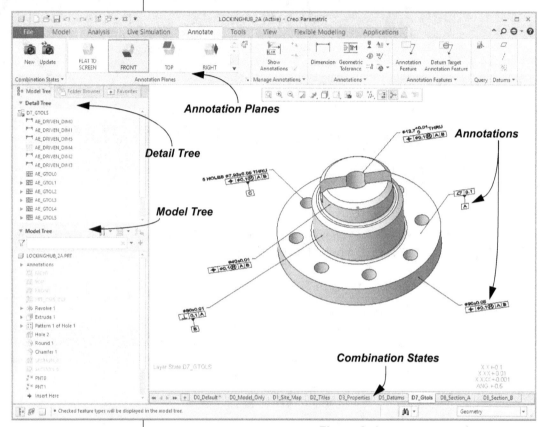

Figure 2–1

2.2 Annotate Tab

The *Annotate* tab in the ribbon contains the functions used to annotate your models. The ribbon is divided into various groups.

Combination States

Combination states enable you to store views of the model that show required annotations in specific orientations with applicable simplified representations, cross sections, and layer states.

The Combination States group, shown in Figure 2–2, is used to create a new combination state or update the orientation of an existing one.

Figure 2–2

The  (New) option is not the most ideal method for creating new combination states. The preferred method is through the View Manager, as discussed in the *Combination States* section.

Annotation Planes

The Annotation Planes group, shown in Figure 2–3, actives an annotation plane. There are several predefined annotation planes, but you can also create custom ones. The active annotation plane defines the initial annotation orientation for newly created annotations.

Figure 2–3

Manage Annotations

The Manage Annotations group, shown in Figure 2–4, is used to show annotations in the model, add or remove annotations in combination states, or erase annotations from display. These options are also available in the shortcut menu.

Figure 2–4

Annotation Features

The Annotation Features group, shown in Figure 2–5, is used to create annotation features, which are collections of annotation elements such as Dimensions, Notes, Datum Feature Symbols, Geometric Tolerances, etc.

You can also create Datum Target annotation features.

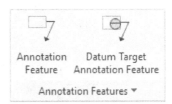

Figure 2–5

Semantic Query

The (Semantic Query) option, shown in Figure 2–6, is used to display and analyze the semantic relationships available for selected annotations.

Figure 2–6

Datums

The Datums group, shown in Figure 2–7, provides tools to create datum planes, axes and points, and sketched datum curves.

Figure 2–7

Annotations

The Annotations group, shown in Figure 2–8, is used to create annotation elements, such as geometric tolerances, driven dimensions, notes, and symbols.

Figure 2–8

In the next several chapters, you will note that it is best practice to create annotation elements in annotation features and not as standalone annotations.

2.3 Annotations and Annotation Features

You can use the Annotations group in the ribbon to create individual annotations, such as notes, geometric tolerances, symbols, etc. The annotations will display in the Detail Tree and in the Annotations group at the top of the Model Tree, as shown in Figure 2–9.

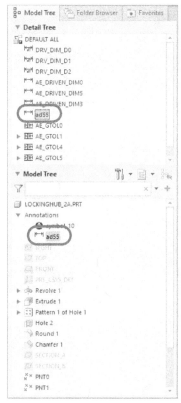

Figure 2–9

Any annotations created outside of an annotation feature is placed in the Annotations group in the Model Tree. Annotations created in or moved into an annotation feature only display in the Detail Tree.

- An annotation feature is a collection of one or more annotation elements, which consist of the annotation name, the annotation itself, the geometric references, and any associated parameters. Annotation features can be redefined to add or remove annotation elements.

- Annotations elements can be created from inside the Annotation Feature dialog box, or they can be selected from existing annotations. If an existing annotation is selected to be part of an annotation feature, it is removed from the Annotations group in the Model Tree.

- Annotation features display in the Model Tree in the order in which they are created, but many companies move them to the regeneration footer, as discussed in the *Detail Tree* section.

- For organizational purposes, annotation features should be created while in the combination state in which they are to be used, and should be named the same as the combination state.

2.4 Combination States

With combination states, you can combine model orientation, simplified representation, appearance state, cross section, and layer state into a single view. For assemblies, you can also combine explode and style states. Creating multiple combination states provides multiple representations of the annotated model. These representations can be used to support the various downstream users of your model and can be output to 3D PDF. The combination states are listed at the bottom of the Creo Parametric window, as shown in Figure 2–10.

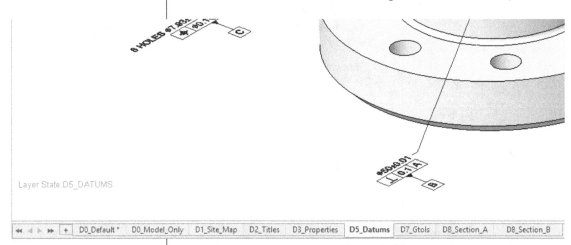

Figure 2–10

- To create a combination state, click 🖿 (View Manager) in the In-graphics toolbar. Select the *All* tab and click **New**. The system adds the combination state to the list with a default name (**Comb0001**, **Comb0002**, etc.) Type a new name and press <Enter>.

- The New Presentation State dialog box displays as shown in Figure 2–11.

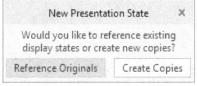

Figure 2–11

- You can use **Reference Originals** so that your new combination state refers to whatever Section, Layer, and Orientation states that were used in the active state.

- Alternatively, use **Create Copies** to copy the Layer and Orientation states under new names. Sections will always reference the originals.

- To rename the combination state, right-click it and select **Rename**.

Naming Convention

Models are created using a standard start part or start assembly. The start part has several predefined states. Although each organization will have a unique naming convention for combination states, you typically would use a convention similar, but not limited, to the following:

- **D0_Model_Only**: Although it is not required for MBD, this state can be used to quickly hide all annotations, displaying only the model.

- **D0_Default:** Security marking, distribution level, revision, data completeness state. **Note** Once created, right-click on the state and select **Make Default** so that the model always opens with this state active.

- **D1_Site_Map:** Notes identifying all available combination states. This is often optional.

- **D2_Titles:** Title Block information (Company name, design description, model number, cage code, design signatures, block tolerances, material and finish requirements). **Note:** Companies publishing the same information in their 3D PDF may not create this state.

- **D3_Properties:** Overall boundary dimensions.

- **D5_Datums:** Datum Feature Symbols.

- **D6_Explode:** Exploded views and unique assembly views.

- **D7_User_Defined:** Define the details of specific features using annotations.

- **D8_Section:** Section views.

Multiple states may be required to fully annotate the model. For example, you may have several user-defined views. To name these combination states correctly, add a letter after the number in the name. For example, **D7A_Front**, **D7B_Top**, and **D7C_Left** might be three custom states you need in your model.

Combination State Elements

To define the attributes of the state, right-click on the name of the state and select **Redefine**. This opens the combination state dialog box, as shown in Figure 2–12.

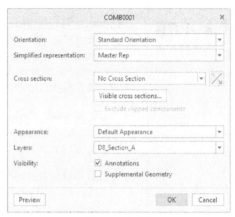

Figure 2–12

Here you can select the orientation, simplified representation, cross section, and layer state that apply to the view. The drop-down lists are populated by the applicable entities stored in the model. For example, the Orientation drop-down list is populated by the Named Views in the model.

If the appropriate view objects are not available in the model, you can create them by right-clicking on the combination state tab and selecting **Display Customization**. You can also select the

View tab and click (View Manager), or click (View Manager) in the In-graphics toolbar. These methods open the View Manager dialog box shown in Figure 2–13.

Figure 2–13

The View Manager dialog box gives you the ability to create simplified representations, sections, layer states, and orientations that can then be selected in the Combination State dialog box.

Annotations added while a combination state is active will only be added to that state. However, you can add annotations to any state using ⁺⁺ (Add to State) in the Manage Annotations group. Conversely, you can remove annotations from any state by selecting them and clicking ⁻⁺ (Remove from State). You can also select either of these options by right-clicking the annotation in the Model Tree or Detail Tree.

2.5 Annotation Planes

Annotation planes are used to establish the plane and orientation of annotations relative to the 3D model. Annotations are not actually placed on the annotation plane, but rather on an imaginary plane that is parallel to and in the same direction as the annotation plane. The actual location of this plane is dependent on the first selected attachment for the annotation. There are predefined annotation planes in the Annotation Planes gallery, as shown in Figure 2–14.

Figure 2–14

Any annotations created after selecting an annotation plane will be created parallel to that plane. When the model is reoriented, the annotations will "follow" the annotation plane. You can add annotations while in 3D orientation, or you can use (Active Annotation Plane) to orient the model in a planar view.

The one exception to that is the (FLAT TO SCREEN) option. With this option, annotations will remain in a fixed orientation so that even if the model is reoriented, they will not move.

Additionally, when (FLAT TO SCREEN) is selected, the (Active Annotation Plane) option is grayed-out. Not all annotations can be placed using this option. For example, you cannot create a dimension with Flat to Screen as the active annotation plane, but you can place notes.

Many organizations choose not to allow the (FLAT TO SCREEN) option, as it does not translate well to 3D PDF.

You can also create custom annotation planes by selecting the arrow, as shown in Figure 2–15.

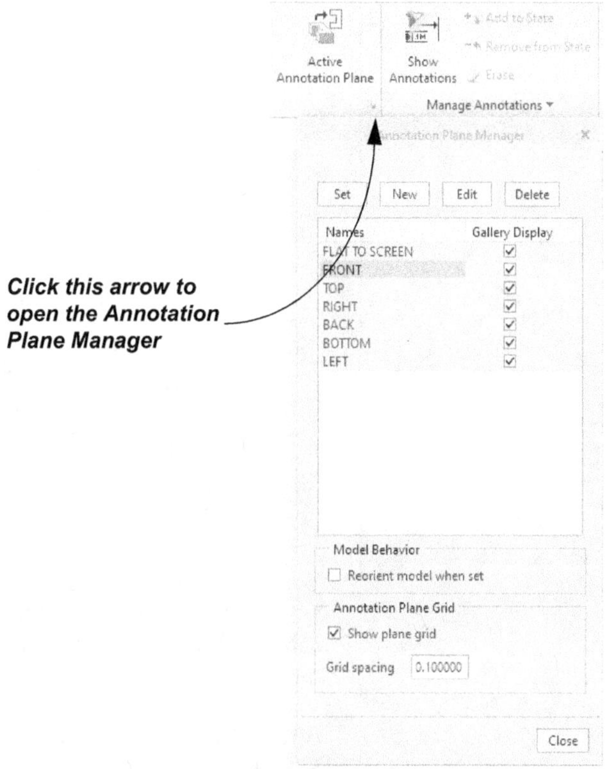

Click this arrow to open the Annotation Plane Manager

Figure 2–15

You can use the Annotation Plane Manager dialog box to set the current annotation plane, create a new annotation plane, or edit or delete an existing annotation plane. You can also remove views from the Annotation Plane gallery by removing the check next to the names in the *Gallery Display* column.

To orient the model automatically when the annotation plane is selected, enable **Reorient model when set**.

When you create a new annotation plane, the Annotation Plane Definition dialog box displays, as shown in Figure 2–16.

Figure 2–16

You can enter a name for the annotation plane, noting that spaces and special characters are not allowed, then select the reference type, which can be either a plane, an existing named model orientation, or flat to screen.

Alternatively, you can select an existing annotation and the system will use the annotation plane that was used to create the annotation selected.

When you define an annotation plane, you not only select the plane to which the annotation will be parallel, but also the direction in which the text will be displayed.The system displays a blue arrow indicating the viewing direction, and a red arrow indicating the direction in which annotations will be created, as shown in Figure 2–17.

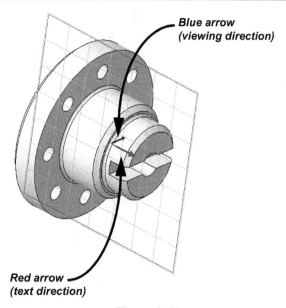

**Blue arrow
(viewing direction)**

**Red arrow
(text direction)**

Figure 2–17

You can click **Flip** to flip the viewing direction and change the angle of the text rotation.

2.6 Detail Tree

Annotation features do not have geometry and, therefore, cannot be selected in the graphics area. If you select an annotation belonging to an annotation feature, it is only that one element you are selecting.

To be certain, you can select annotation features and toggle on their display in the Model Tree. Click ⊤ ˅ (Settings) in the Model Tree and click **Tree Filters**. In the Model Tree Items dialog box, enable **Annotations**, as shown in Figure 2–18. This option can be set by default using a **tree.cfg** file.

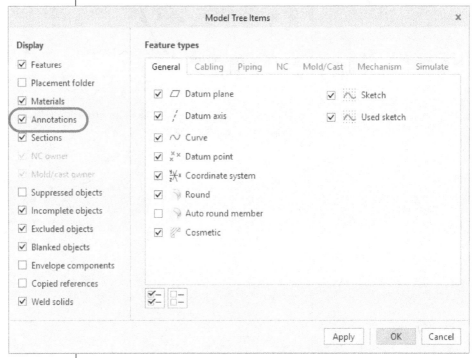

Figure 2–18

When you enter Annotate mode, the system displays the Detail Tree in addition to the Model Tree, as shown in Figure 2–19.

Figure 2–19

Annotations are added to the model as stand alone annotations or as multiple annotation elements comprising annotation features. In either case, the individual elements are listed in the Detail Tree and are grouped together based on annotation type.

Annotations include geometric tolerances and dimensions, but also non-dimensional annotations such as notes and surface finish symbols.

Dimensions listed as **DRV_DIM_D#** are shown dimensions, or in other words, dimensions used to create the 3D model geometry.

You can also manually create dimensions. These are considered driven dimensions (driven by the model's geometry) and are listed as **ad#** in the Detail Tree.

- If you create a dimension as part of an annotation feature, or select a driven dimension, right-click, and select **Create Annotation Feature**, it will be listed as **AE_DRIVEN_DIM#**.

In the Model Tree section, created dimensions, notes, geometric tolerances, etc. that are not otherwise in an annotation feature, are listed under the Annotations folder, as shown in Figure 2–20.

Figure 2–20

Annotation features display in the Model Tree such as any other feature. They should be renamed to match their associated annotation feature, and can be redefined, edited, deleted, and so on. An example is shown in Figure 2–21.

Figure 2–21

Regeneration Footer

Since annotations features are driven by the geometry, a common practice is to place them in the regeneration footer. The regeneration footer is a section of the Model Tree that lists certain types of features, referred to as *Declaration* features. *Declaration* features do not affect the model's geometry and essentially reference the model's final geometry.

These include zones, datum reference features, annotation features, etc. You should move an annotation feature to the footer by right-clicking it and selecting **Move to footer**. An example is shown in Figure 2–22.

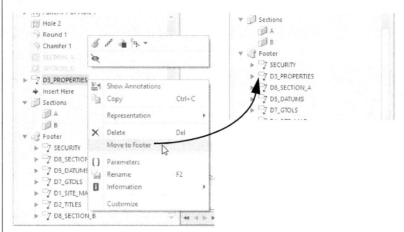

Figure 2–22

Practice 2a

Investigate the Annotation Interface

Practice Objectives

- Open an annotated model.
- Review the Model Tree, Detail Tree, and set of combination states.

In this practice, you investigate the annotation interface using an annotated model that has combination states, annotations such as geometric tolerances, and dimensions. The tools for annotating a 3D model are found in the *Annotate* tab of the ribbon, as shown in Figure 2–23.

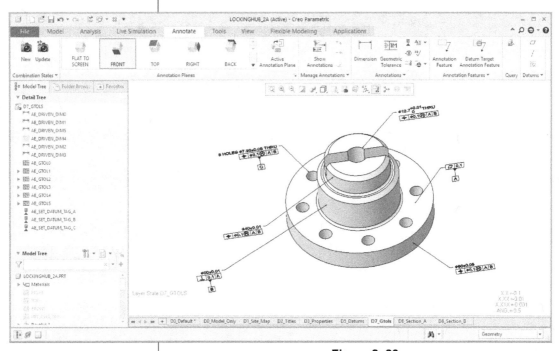

Figure 2–23

Task 1 - Open the part file.

1. If required, click ⬚ (Select Working Directory), navigate to the *Creo Parametric Model Based Definition Practice Files* folder and click **OK**.

2. Open **lockinghub_2a.prt**.

3. In the In-graphics toolbar, apply the following initial setup:

    *   ✖ (Datum Display Filters): All off
    *   ⬜ (Display Style): ⬜ (Shading With Edges)
    *   ⬛ (Annotation Display): Enabled
    *   ⤳ (Spin Center): Disabled

    The model displays as shown in Figure 2–24.

The Default All state displays by default. All annotations display in the other states.

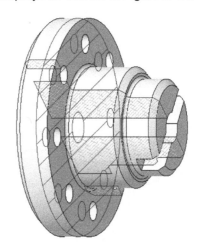

Figure 2–24

Task 2 - Investigate the Model Tree.

The annotation features display at the bottom of the Model Tree.

1. In the Model Tree, click ⯗ ˅ (Settings).

2. Click **Tree Filters** and select **Annotations** from the Display list, if not already selected.

3. Click **OK** and the Model Tree displays as shown in Figure 2–25.

Figure 2–25

4. Expand the **Footer** node, then expand several of the annotation features to display the elements comprising them. The **D5_DATUMS** annotation feature is shown expanded in Figure 2–26.

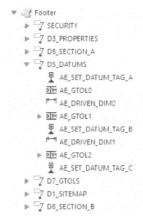

Figure 2–26

Task 3 - Investigate the Detail Tree.

1. In the ribbon, select the *Annotate* tab. The Model Tree slides down to display the Detail Tree, as shown in Figure 2–27.

The annotations were added to the other combination states, so initially the Detail Tree displays as empty.

Figure 2–27

2. In the tabs at the bottom of the Creo Parametric window, select the *D0_Default* combination state. The model displays, as shown in Figure 2–28.

STATE: PRELIMINARY

DESTRUCTION NOTICE
DESTROY BY ANY METHOD THAT WILL PREVENT DISCLOSURE
OF CONTENTS OR RECONSTRUCTION OF THE DOCUMENT

DISTRIBUTION: C
DISTRIBUTION AUTHORIZED TO U.S. GOVERNMENT AGENCIES ONLY AND THEIR CONTRACTORS

WARNING
THIS DOCUMENT CONTAINS TECHNICAL DATA WHOSE EXPORT IS RESTRICTED

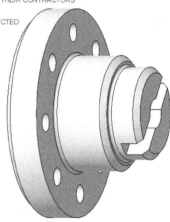

Figure 2–28

3. The Detail Tree updates to reflect the annotation elements, as shown in Figure 2–29.

Figure 2–29

4. In the Detail Tree, select **AE_NOTE0**. The note highlights on the screen as shown in Figure 2–30.

Note that the text highlighted in gray is driven by parameters and relations.

Figure 2–30

5. In the Detail Tree, select **AE_NOTE1**. The note highlights on the screen as shown in Figure 2–31.

Note that the DIST_NOTE, DISTRIBUTION_LEVEL and COMPLETENESS_ STATE parameters are used in the notes.

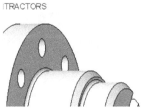

Figure 2–31

6. In the ribbon, select the *Tools* tab.

7. Click [ ] (Parameters). The Parameters dialog box opens as shown in Figure 2–32.

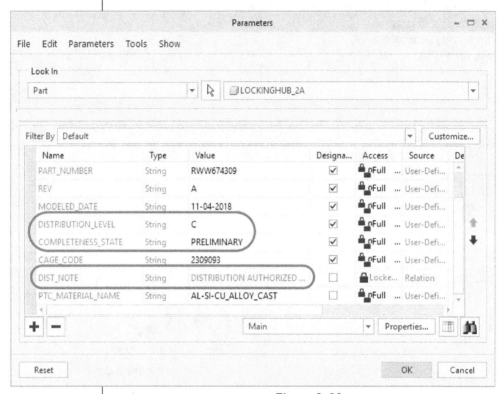

Figure 2–32

8. Close the Parameters dialog box.

9. In the *Tools* tab, click d= (Relations). The Relations dialog box opens as shown in Figure 2–33.

The relations set the value of the DIST_ NOTE parameter based on the value of the DISTRIBUTION_LEVEL parameter.

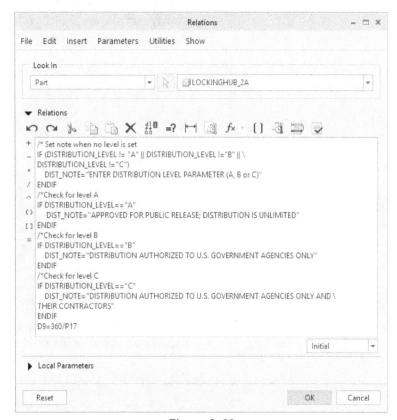

Figure 2–33

10. Close the Relations dialog box.

11. In the ribbon, select the *Annotate* tab.

Task 4 - Investigate the other combination states.

1. Select the *D0_Model_Only* combination state tab. The model displays as shown in Figure 2–34.

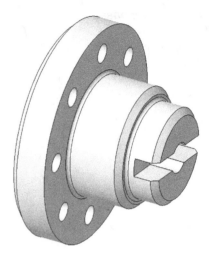

Figure 2–34

2. Select the *D1_Site_Map* combination state tab. The model displays as shown in Figure 2–35.

SITE MAP

D0_DEFAULT: Security marking, distribution level, revision, data completeness state

D0_MODEL_ONLY: View of model Only

D1_SITE_MAP: Notes identifying all available combination states

D2_TITLES: Title Block information

D3_PROPERTIES: Overall boundary dimensions

D5_DATUMS: View of model with Datum Feature Symbols

D7_GTOLS: View to display geometric tolerances

D8_SECTION_A: Section view of the holes

D8_SECTION_B: Section view through the model

Figure 2–35

3. Select the *D2_Titles* combination state tab. The model displays as shown in Figure 2–36.

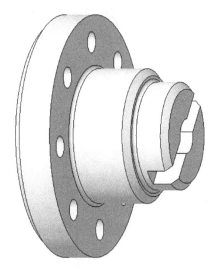

DESCRIPTION: Aluminum locking hub
MODEL: RWW674309
MODELED BY: S.HENDREN
DATE: 11-04-2018
REVISION: A
CAGE CODE: 2309093

Figure 2–36

4. Select the *D3_Properties* combination state tab. The model displays as shown in Figure 2–37.

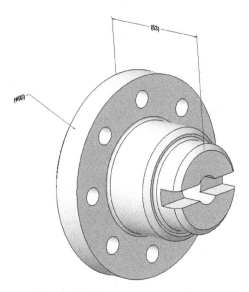

Figure 2–37

5. Select the *D5_Datums* combination state tab. The model displays as shown in Figure 2–38.

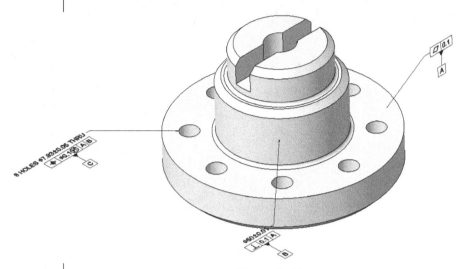

Figure 2–38

6. Select the *D7_Gtols* combination state tab. The model displays as shown in Figure 2–39.

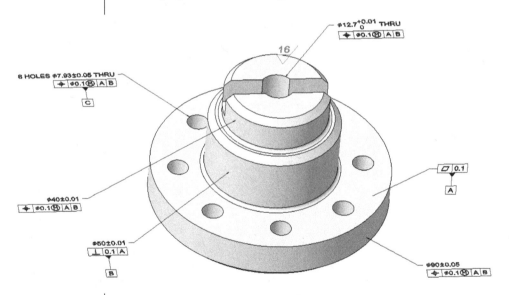

Figure 2–39

7. Select the *D8_Section_A* combination state tab. The model displays as shown in Figure 2–40.

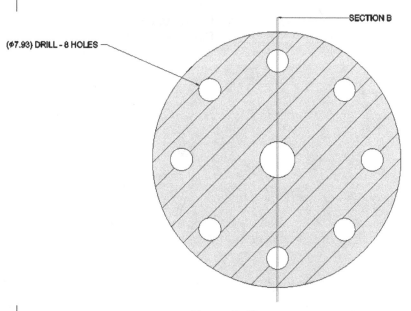

Figure 2–40

8. Select the *D8_Section_B* combination state tab. The model displays as shown in Figure 2–41.

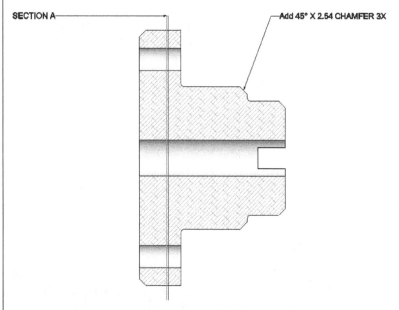

Figure 2–41

9. Select the *D7_Gtols* combination state tab.

Task 5 - Investigate the annotation planes.

1. Place the cursor over 🔻 (BOTTOM) from the Annotation Planes group in the ribbon and notice the grid that displays, as shown in Figure 2–42.

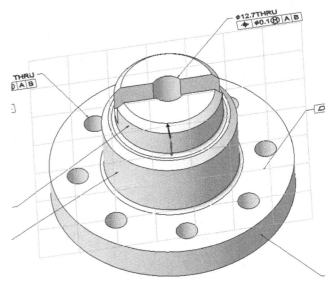

Figure 2–42

2. Click 🔻 (BOTTOM) and click 🔲 (Active Annotation Plane) to orient the model parallel to the screen, as shown in Figure 2–43.

Figure 2–43

3. Click ◢ (RIGHT) and click ⬚ (Active Annotation Plane) to orient the model parallel to the screen, as shown in Figure 2–44.

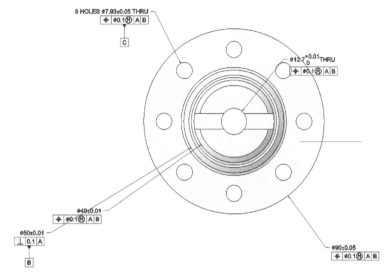

Figure 2–44

4. Click the *D7_Gtols* combination state tab to reset the orientation.

5. Place the cursor over ◢ (FLAT TO SCREEN) and notice the annotation plane grid, as shown in Figure 2–45. Annotations added when FLAT TO SCREEN is used will remain parallel to the screen regardless of changes to the model orientation.

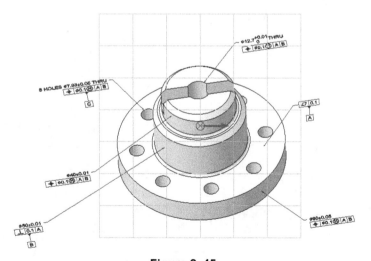

Figure 2–45

6. Click 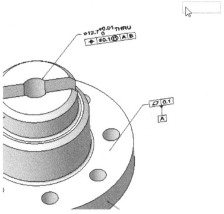 (FLAT TO SCREEN).

7. In the Annotations group, click (Note).

8. Click the location shown in Figure 2–46 to place the note.

Figure 2–46

9. Type **Engineering to review hole pattern** in the text box.

10. Click on the screen twice to complete the note.

11. Spin the model and note that the note does not move and remains parallel to the screen, as shown in Figure 2–47.

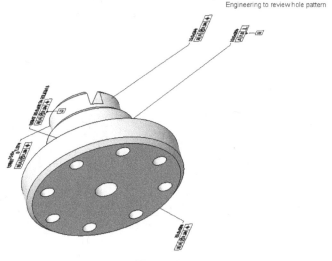

Figure 2–47

12. Select the note you just created and notice that it highlights in the Detail Tree and Model Tree, as shown in Figure 2–48.

Figure 2–48

13. In the Manage Annotations group in the ribbon, click ⁻⁺ (Remove from State) to remove it from display.

14. The note is removed from the Detail Tree list, but it still displays in the Model Tree, under the *Annotations* listing, as shown in Figure 2–49.

Figure 2–49

15. Right-click on the note and select **Delete**. Click **Yes** to confirm.

16. Close the model and erase it from session.

Chapter Review Questions

1. Combination states store views of the model that show required annotations with applicable _____.

    a. Simplified Representations

    b. Orientations

    c. Layer States

    d. Cross Sections

    e. All of the above

2. When redefining a combination state, the Orientation drop-down list is populated with objects from the _____ list.

    a. Named Views

    b. Orientation

    c. View State

    d. Display Style

3. Annotations are not placed on the annotation plane itself, but rather on an imaginary plane parallel to the annotation plane.

    a. True

    b. False

4. Dimensions created (not shown) using the annotation tools display in the Detail Tree with the _____ format.

    a. DRV_DIM_D#

    b. ad#

    c. DIM#

    d. DIM_DRIVEN#

5. Annotation features are collections of annotation elements and are displayed in the Model Tree like other features.

    a. True

    b. False

Answers: 1.e, 2.a, 3.a, 4.d, 5.a

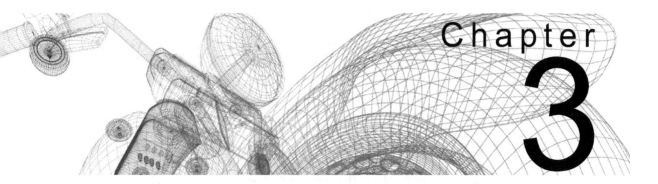

Preparing the Model

This chapter covers several preparations necessary to prepare your models for Model-Based Definition. Many of the topics covered will already be set up in your environment, but it is important to know how they were set up and why. You will learn to establish start parts with predefined parameters, layers, and views. The configuration options and detailing options related to annotations will also be discussed.

Learning Objectives in This Chapter

- Review configuration options applicable to 3D annotations.
- Understand how to work with parameters in 3D annotations.
- Understand how to use layers, sections, and view states with combination states.
- Understand how start parts can be used to set up a consistent modeling environment

3.1 Configuration Options

Configuration Options

There are two configuration files that can affect how annotations display in your Creo Parametric session: **config.pro** and **model.dtl**.

The **config.pro** file controls your design environment, and is session specific, meaning it must be present when Creo Parametric is launched, or loaded after it is launched. Although there are many options that can affect annotations, several options are described as follows:

Option	Description	Available Values
display_annotations	Controls whether annotations display in 3D models or not.	yes (default) no
intf3d_out_anno_as	Determines if annotations are exported, and if so, whether they are exported as polyline or semantic.	graphic (default) semantic none default
tol_display	Displays dimensions with or without tolerances.	no (default) yes
gtol_dim_placement	Controls the display of geometric tolerances in Part mode.	on_bottom (default) under_value
restricted_gtol_dialog	Determines if the Geometric Tolerance dialog grays out elements considered "illegal" relative to the tolerance being created.	yes (default) no
tolerance_standard	Sets the tolerance standard used when creating the model.	ansi (default) iso
model_detail_options_file	Points to the Detail options file that sets the detailing options for models.	Enter the path to the detail options file, for example "C:\configurations\3d_parts.dtl"

To edit the **config.pro** file, click **File>Options**, and click **Configuration Editor** in the PTC Creo Parametric Options dialog box, as shown in Figure 3–1.

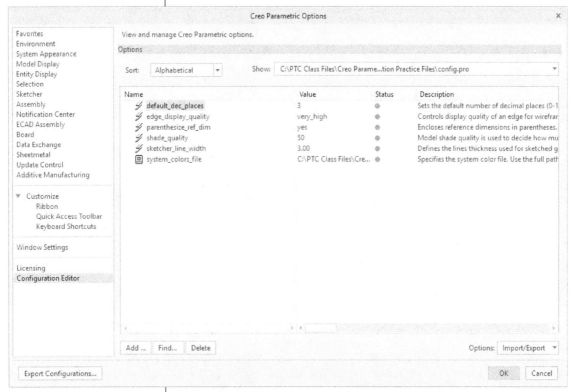

Figure 3–1

If you know the option you want to set, you can click **Add** and type the name of the option in the Add Options dialog box. As you type, the system fills in the *Option name* field with the configuration option that matches what you enter, as shown in Figure 3–2.

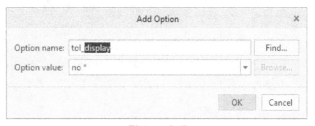

Figure 3–2

If you are unsure of the option, you can click **Find** in either the Creo Parametric Options or Options dialog boxes, and the system displays the Find Option dialog box, as shown in Figure 3–3.

Figure 3–3

You can use wild-cards such as * to help your search. You will find that you can receive more results by enabling the Search descriptions option as well. This forces the system to look for the keyword in the option's description and its name.

Once you have the option you want, select or type the **Set value**, then click **Add / Change** to add the option to the **config.pro** file.

When you finish adding and editing entries, you will be prompted with a warning dialog box, asking if you want to save the settings to a configuration file, as shown in Figure 3–4.

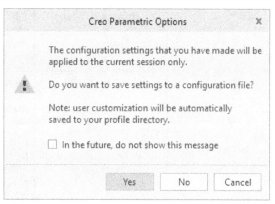

Figure 3–4

If you click **Yes**, you can save the configuration file to your startup directory so that it is automatically loaded every time you start Creo Parametric. If you click **No**, the settings will only apply to this session, and will revert to the previous set of options the next time you start Creo Parametric.

Detail Options

The Detail options add additional controls to the characteristics of objects such as geometric tolerance standards, arrow display, text heights, and so on. The file specified in the **config.pro** option **model_detail_options_file** contains the detail settings for new models.

Unlike the **config.pro** file, which pertains to a Creo Parametric session, the **model.dtl** file is pulled into and stored with the model, in the same way the drawing.dtl file follows a 2D drawing. Most of the options found in the **model.dtl** file are the same as those found in the **drawing.dtl** file, with some options being specific to 3D models.

Several metric Detail options are listed as follows:

Option	Description	Available Values
arrow_style	Controls the arrow head style for all detail objects requiring arrows.	closed (default) open filled
arrow_length_ratio	Sets the length of leader line arrow heads as 0.6 * the calculated text height. (3D Only)	0.600000 (default) user-defined value

arrow_width_ratio	Sets the width of leader line arrow heads as 0.2 * the calculated text height. (3D Only)	0.200000 (default) user-defined value
decimal_marker	Specifies the character used to indicate a decimal point in secondary dimensions.	comma_for_metric_dual (default) period comma
default_tolerance_display_style	Controls the spacing and vertical justification of tolerance values relative to the nominal dimension according to ASME or ISO standards.	std_asme (default) std_iso
default_tolerance_mode	Sets the default tolerance mode for newly created dimensions.	nominal (default) limits plusminus plusminussym plusminussym_super
set_datum_triangle_display	Determines the set datum triangle style.	filled (default) open
set_datum_leader_length_ratio	Sets the default length of the leader for a draft set datum or model set datum. (3D Only)	2.070000 (default) user-defined value
text_height	Sets the text height, calculated based upon the size of the model envelope when the annotation is created. (3D Only)	calculated (default) user-defined value
witness_line_delta_ratio	Sets the extension of the witness line beyond the dimension leader arrows. (3D Only)	0.600000 (default) user-defined value
witness_line_offset_ratio	Sets the offset between a dimension line and object being dimensioned and controls the size of the line break at the intersection of witness lines. (3D Only)	0.300000 (default) user-defined value

To edit the Detail options, click **File>Prepare>Model Properties**, which opens the Model Properties dialog box, as shown in Figure 3–5.

Figure 3–5

Click **change** for the Detail Options row and the system opens the Options dialog box, as shown in Figure 3–6.

Figure 3–6

The find function works in the same manner as it does for the configuration files. You can also select an option in the list, and the *Option* and *Value* areas display. You then select the *Value* from the drop-down list, as shown in Figure 3–7.

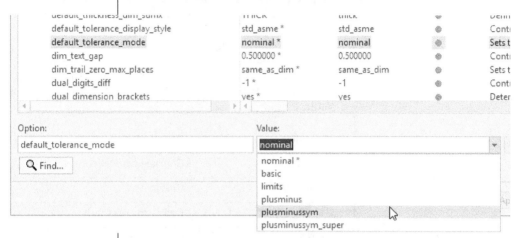

Figure 3–7

Once the appropriate options are set and you click **OK**, the options are written to the model. You can also save the file for use in other models by clicking (Save Configuration). You can load a Detail file by clicking (Open Configuration).

3.2 Parameters

To facilitate Model-Based Definition, a minimum amount of meta-data must be stored in the model. Your company will have the required parameters established in start models, and should have them outlined in an MBD Schema.

There are many required parameters, and they will vary by organization, but an example list is found in the table below. Your organization will use similar parameters, although the names might differ.

Parameter	Description
CHK_DATE	Checked date
CHK_NAME	Checked by
CAGE_CODE	Cage code number
PART_NUMBER	Part number
MODELED_DATE	Date of part creation
MODELED_BY	Part creator
DESCRIPTION	General model description
LEGAL_NOTES	General legal or contractual notes
MATERIAL	General note for material
MATL_TYPE	Material type
MODEL_NUMBER	Product model number
REV	Revision level
REV_DATE	Date of latest revision approval
UNIT_WEIGHT	Weight of part for BOMs
DISTRIBUTION_LEVEL	Used to define notes indicating how the model can be distributed
COMPLETENESS_STATE	Define where the model is in the design process (e.g. Preliminary, In Review, etc.)
VOLUME	Product volume

To access the model parameters, select the *Tools* tab, then click [] (Parameters) in the Model Parameters group to open the Parameters dialog box, as shown in Figure 3–8.

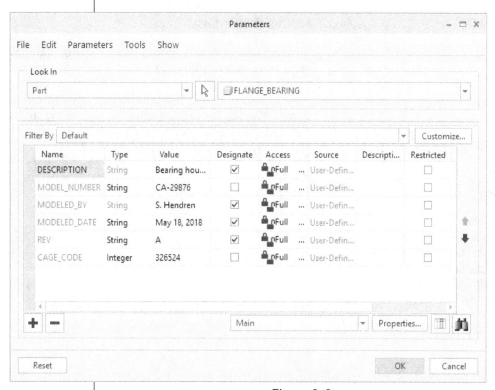

Figure 3–8

The parameter values can be edited as required from model to model, and they can be of Type: Integer, Real Number, String or Yes No.

It is important to **Designate** the parameters defined by your organization, to ensure they are readable by downstream tools and for use as attributes in your PLM system. Your company will have rules regarding the parameters to be designated, and who will be responsible for setting the values.

3.3 Layers

Layers are used to manage the display of entities in your models. For MBD, layers can be used to support model display for combination views.

You can use layers to control the display of your annotations, including dimensions, notes, etc., so you can show or hide them as required using Layer States in the various combination views. Having said that, most organizations only use Layer States to control the display of supplemental geometry, such as axes, curves (sketches), and surfaces (designated areas).

A standard naming convention should be employed to identify the layers. In the example Layer Tree shown in Figure 3–9, the naming convention is D#_Description.

Your company will have its own set of layers with its own naming convention.The Layer Names should coincide where possible with Combination View names.

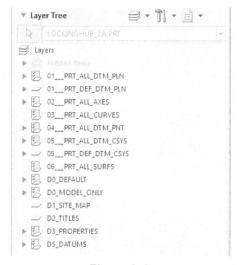

Figure 3–9

Objects can be manually added to layers, or you can setup rules to automatically add them. For example, to add a rule to automatically place set datums to the **D5_DATUMS** layer, right-click on the layer in the layer tree, and select **Layer Properties**. In the Layer Properties dialog box, select the *Rules* tab, as shown in Figure 3–10.

Press **Edit Rules** to open the Rule Editor dialog box. Here, you can select **Annotation Element** from the Look for drop-down list, set the Attributes *Rule* to **Type**, and select **Datum Feature Symbol** from the Value drop-down list, as shown in Figure 3–11.

Figure 3–10

Figure 3–11

When you add rules, select the **Associative** option from the Options drop-down list in the Layer Properties dialog box to ensure annotations meeting the rule criteria are automatically placed on the layer. If the **Associative** option is not selected, new annotations will not automatically be impacted by the rules.

3.4 Sections

You can create sections in your model to cut away and look at the interior details, as shown in Figure 3–12.

Figure 3–12

Sections can be created from the *View* tab by clicking the

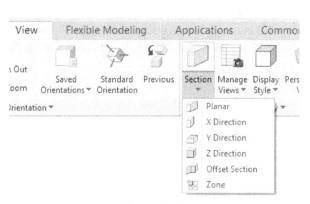 (Section) menu, as shown in Figure 3–13. Alternatively, if you are in the View Manager dialog box, you can select the *Sections* tab, click **New**, and select the type of section you want to create, as shown in Figure 3–14.

Figure 3–13

Figure 3–14

There are six types of sections you can create, listed as follows:

Section Type	Description
Planar	Create a cross section by referencing a plane, point or flat surface.
X Direction	Create a cross section by referencing the X-Axis of the default coordinate system.
Y Direction	Create a cross section by referencing the Y-Axis of the default coordinate system.
Z Direction	Create a cross section by referencing the Z-Axis of the default coordinate system.
Offset	Create a cross section by referencing a sketch.
Zone	Create a 3D cross section established by a zone.

At the time of writing, several tools for viewing MBD data, Creo View and 3D PDF among them, have limited, if any, support for sections other than Planar and X, Y and Z Direction sections. As such, you will only cover those section types in this course.

Although there are separate commands to initiate Planar, X Direction, Y Direction and Z Direction sections, they all use the same interface. In fact, regardless of the type you start with, you can create any of the other types by selecting the appropriate reference.

For example, when you click **Planar**, the system displays the Section dashboard, shown in Figure 3–15.

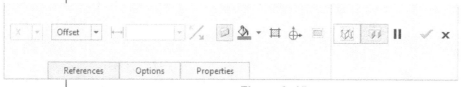

Figure 3–15

You select a planar surface, datum plane, or datum point as a reference, and the system creates a cut through the model to reveal the interior section. The **FRONT** datum plane is selected to establish the section location, as shown in Figure 3–16.

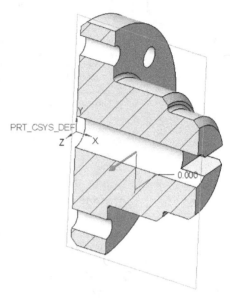

Figure 3–16

However, if you select a coordinate system instead, you immediately switch to the creation of an X Direction section, as shown in Figure 3–17.

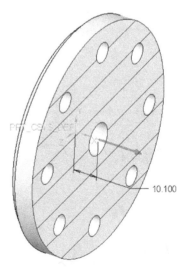

Figure 3–17

You can then use the drop-down list from the dashboard to change to a **Y** Direction or **Z** Direction section as required. Should you then select a plane or point reference, the section reverts to a Planar section.

Section Orientation

When creating sections for use in MBD, it is important that the section be created such that material is removed toward the viewing direction, as shown in Figure 3–18. Removing material facing away from the viewing direction is not a typical use case for a cross section.

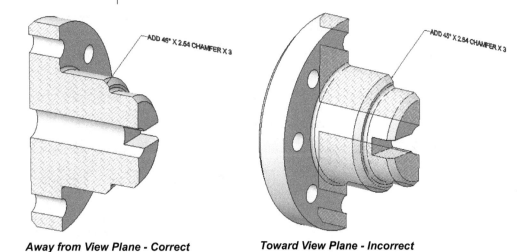

Away from View Plane - Correct   *Toward View Plane - Incorrect*

Figure 3–18

Also, at the time of writing, when you remove material away from the viewing direction, the mirrored section will appear in the 3D PDF and annotations may be missing.

Section Dashboard Options

In the dashboard, you can use the options shown in the table below for any of the planar section types:

Option	Description
 ⊢⊣ 0.00 ▾	Enter the distance to offset the section from the selected reference. Note that you can also drag the arrow in the graphics window.
⟋	Flip the clipping direction of the section.
▱	Cap the section by displaying a surface over the section. Disable this to see the internal geometry that lies beyond the section plane.
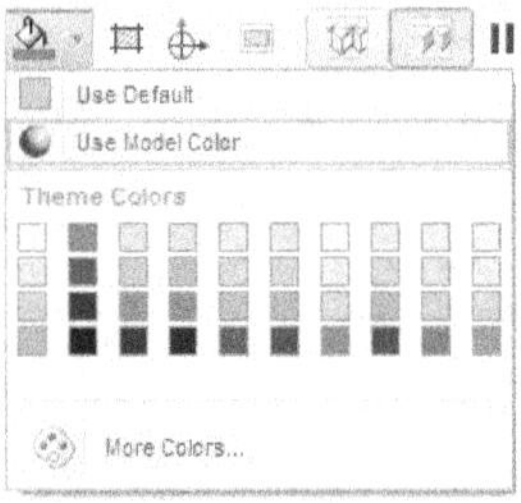	Change the color of the capped surface. Note that Creo View will only use the model color, regardless of what you select here.
▱	Display the hatch pattern on the surface of the section.
⊕→	Enable the free positioning of the clipping plane, so that you might translate and rotate the clipping plane as required.
▭	Display a 2D view of the section in a separate sub-window.

Sections are listed at the end of the Model Tree, as shown in Figure 3–19.

You can edit the hatching by right-clicking the section in the Model Tree and selecting **Edit Hatching**. The Edit Hatching dialog box displays, as shown in Figure 3–20.

Figure 3–19   **Figure 3–20**

Here, you can set the hatch pattern from ANSI or ISO standard libraries, edit the angle, scale, and so on.It should be noted that, since the hatching is a purely visual characteristic, it is not required to edit it for MBD.

Section Plane Callouts

Some organizations will use callouts for section view planes. To call out the section in other views, you must create a datum point on the section plane and attach a note to it. This process is covered in *Chapter 5*.

3.5 Explode States (Assembly Only)

Creo Parametric enables you to create exploded views of assemblies. By customizing the exploded positions of the components, you can create a view that can be used in a drawing to indicate an assembly procedure.

To create a temporary explode, click

(Exploded View) in the Model Display group, in the Model tab. The model displays in its default exploded position and can be modified by dynamically dragging components to new positions in the view. Click the icon again to revert the assembly back to its assembled state.

To create a customized explode click (View Manager) in the Model Display group in the *Model* tab or in the In-graphics toolbar and then select the *Explode* tab, as shown in Figure 3–21.

Figure 3–21

Click **New** in the *Explode* area in the View Manager dialog box. Enter a name for the explode and press <Enter>. The new explode is now active, as indicated by the arrow.

Click **Properties** to define the view properties. The View
Manager dialog box opens as shown in Figure 3–22.

View Manager			×
Simp Rep	Style	Sections	Layers
Explode	Orient	Appearance	All

Item	Status

Remove

<< List	Close

Figure 3–22

Click ⚒ (Edit Position) to open the *Explode Tool* dashboard, as
shown in Figure 3–23. Use the options in the dialog box to define
the component positions or use the arrows in the view window to
move the component in the required direction.

Translate   **Rotate**   **View Plane**

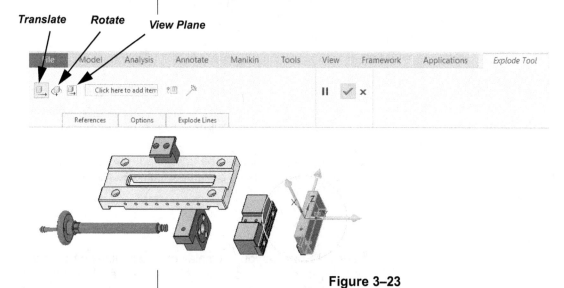

Figure 3–23

For example, a planar surface can be selected as the motion reference when repositioning a component in an exploded assembly view. The component is then restricted to move in a direction that is parallel to the planar motion reference.

Select the *References* tab to open the Reference panel. Activate the *Movement Reference* area and select an **Axis** or **Straight Edge** as the motion reference.

Click 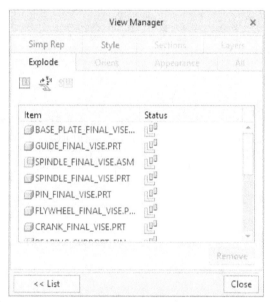 (Translate), (Rotate), or (View Plane) for the type of movement you want. You can also use the arrows in the view window to drag the component. Once you select the component, an arrow displays.

Use the left mouse button to drag the handle and place the component, as required. Once all of the components have been moved, click ✔ (Apply Changes) to close the *Explode Tool* dashboard.

The View Manager dialog box opens as shown in Figure 3–24, displaying a list of exploded components.

View Manager	
Simp Rep	Style	Sections	Layers
Explode	Orient	Appearance	All

Item	Status
BASE_PLATE_FINAL_VISE...	
GUIDE_FINAL_VISE.PRT	
SPINDLE_FINAL_VISE.ASM	
SPINDLE_FINAL_VISE.PRT	
PIN_FINAL_VISE.PRT	
FLYWHEEL_FINAL_VISE.P...	
CRANK_FINAL_VISE.PRT	

<< List   Close

Figure 3–24

Individual components can be un-exploded by selecting them in the View Manager dialog box and clicking **Remove**. Repeat this step, as required.

Offset Lines

Offset lines enable you to display exploding lines when the assembly is in the explode state. The lines help to explain how the assembly components are assembled to one another.

- To create offset lines, click ⚛ (Edit Position). In the *Edit Position* tab, click ⚗ (Offset Lines) and select two references to define the extent of the line. The references can be an axis, surface normal, or edge/curve. Once created, you can modify, delete, or change the line style for the line.

- Click 🖳 (Exploded View) or 🖳 (Un-explode) along the top of the View Manager dialog box to toggle the position of the selected components between the exploded and unexploded states.

- Click 🖳 (Toggle Explode) to only un-explode a selected component. Alternatively, you can remove the component from the explode state.

- Click **List** to return to the explode listing. The current explode is temporarily modified with the new settings and displays with a plus (+) symbol appended to the end of its name. For example, A (+) indicates that the A explode was displayed and that it has been changed.

Explode can also be updated by clicking Edit and selecting Save.

- To update the changes in the model, right-click and select **Save**. The Save Display Elements dialog box opens as shown in Figure 3–25. Click **OK** to finish the save action.

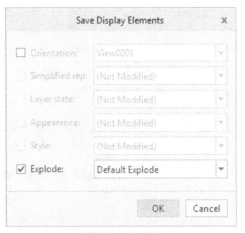

Figure 3–25

*You can also click **Edit** and clear the checkmark next to the **Explode State** option.*

To un-explode the view, right-click in the View Manager dialog box and disable the **Explode** option to clear the checkmark next to the option or click 🖳 (Exploded View) in the Model Display group in the *Model* tab.

3.6 View Manager Options

The View Manager is used to present the model and its annotations to comply with MBD standards. The View Manager enables you to present the model in various conditions, by controlling the simplified representation, cross section, layer states, orientation, etc. The View Manager dialog box is shown in Figure 3–26.

Figure 3–26

View Manager Tabs

Simp Rep

If you are working with an assembly, simplified representations are used to control which assembly components are brought into session and displayed. Part level simplified representations can be used to change the level of detail for specific views of the model.

If the simplified representation you require is not in the model, click **New** and create one from the View Manager.

Sections

You can create cross section views to show internal geometry that cannot otherwise be seen. Existing model sections can be accessed through the *Sections* tab, but you can create new sections there as well.

Layers

Layers states enable you to hide and show layers in different ways, in different states. For example, you might set a layer state where you hide a layer, and in another you might unhide it. When you switch between layer states, the layer status updates automatically.

Orient

The View Manager also provides access to the saved orientations of the model. In addition to the orientations already saved, you can reorient the model and save new orientations. You should provide as many views as required to ensure the model can be fully viewed and understood without manually reorienting it.

Appearance (Does Not Translate to 3D PDF)

You can define different appearance states for a model using the *Appearance* tab in the View Manager dialog box, as shown in Figure 3–27. You can define and switch between different color combinations for your designs.

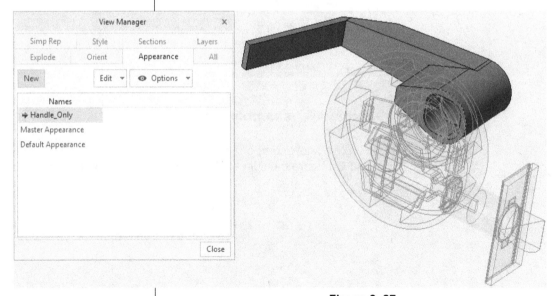

Figure 3–27

Apply appearances to surface, features, or components in your model. In the *Appearance* tab of the View Manager, click **New** and enter a name. You can repeat this for as many different combinations of colors, textures, etc. that you require. This enables you to quickly change the appearance for various use cases.

Style (Assembly Only - Does Not Translate to 3D PDF)

When working with assemblies, you can control the display of individual components, and store the display as a Style state. Figure 3–28 shows the options for display.

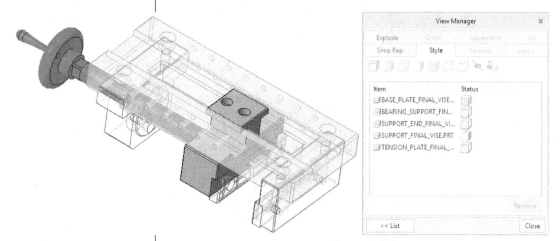

Figure 3–28

Explode (Assembly Only)

You can show components of an assembly in an exploded view, and can store multiple exploded views as Explode states.

3.7 Combination States

You can create views that encompass various combinations of orientations, layer states, simplified representations, and so on, and store them as combination states. They are created using the *All* tab in the View Manager, as shown in Figure 3–29.

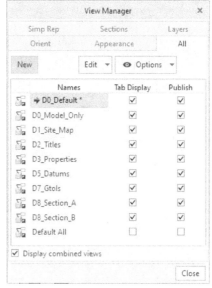

Figure 3–29

You can select a combination state, right-click, and select **Redefine** to open the dialog box. From here, you select the view options you want to apply to this combination state, as shown in Figure 3–30.

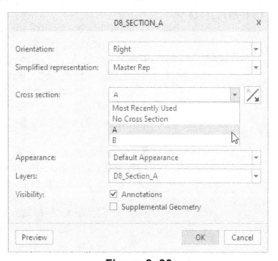

Figure 3–30

Any combination states that have a checkmark in the *Tab Display* column will display at the bottom of the graphics window. You can select the tabs to switch between combination states. If you hover over a tab a preview displays, as shown in Figure 3–31.

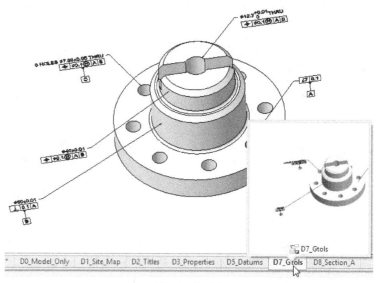

Figure 3–31

Annotations and Supplemental Geometry

Layers can be used to control the visibility of annotations and supplemental geometry. Supplemental geometry includes planes, axes, coordinate systems, points and curves. However, you can also control the display of annotations and supplemental geometry by assigning them directly to a combination state.

The ability to control the visibility of both annotations and supplemental geometry was not available prior to Creo Parametric 4.0. In Creo Parametric 2.0 and 3.0, annotations could be controlled by assignment to a combination state, but supplemental geometry had to be controlled using layers. Prior to Creo Parametric 2.0, both annotations and supplemental geometry could only be controlled by layers.

To ensure compatibility with legacy data and established processes, there are three schemes available for any combination state in the model.

- **MBD State:** Manages the visibility of both annotations and supplemental geometry by direct assignment to a combination state.

- **Semi-MBD State:** Manages the visibility of annotations only by direct assignment to a combination state and to manage the visibility of supplemental geometry by using layers. Since this is the same as the visibility management scheme available in Creo Parametric 2.0 and 3.0, the majority of the combination states in this content use this state, as your company is likely to have MBD data that has already been created.

- **Non-MBD State:** Manages the visibility of both annotations and supplemental geometry by using layers and layer states. This is the same visibility management scheme available prior to Creo Parametric 2.0, and will not be used in the combination states in this content.

The default method of visibility management for newly created combination states is controlled using the configuration option *combined_state_type*, and the available options are **mbd**, **semi_mbd**, and **non_mbd**.

Note that this configuration does not affect combination states created prior to setting it.

The visibility management scheme for each combination state is identified with icons in the combination state tabs at the bottom of the window and in the Detail Tree. For MBD states, the

⑤ icon displays, and for Semi-MBD states, the ⑤ icon displays. Non-MBD states have no icon. An example of the Detail tree for a Semi-MBD state is shown in Figure 3–32.

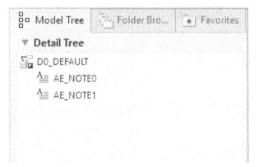

Figure 3–32

You can set the visibility options from the combination state dialog box by selecting the Annotations and/or Supplemental Geometry checkboxes, as shown in Figure 3–33.

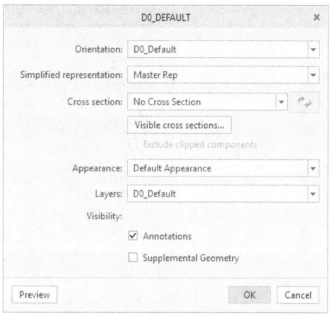

Figure 3–33

Publishing Combination States

In the *All* tab in the View Manager dialog box, you can enable the **Publish** option, which controls the publishing of combination state. You can also select the **Publish** option if you right-click on a combination state tab at the bottom of the Creo Parametric window.

When you enable the **Publish** option, the combination state is published in Creo View. When you clear a checkbox, the combination state is not published in Creo View.

The **Publish** checkbox is selected by default for all new combination states.

3.8 Start Parts

Your company will inevitably have start parts and assemblies for creating models. When you create a new part, the **Use default template** option is selected by default, as shown in Figure 3–34. This tells the system to use the start part you have defined in your **config.pro** file.

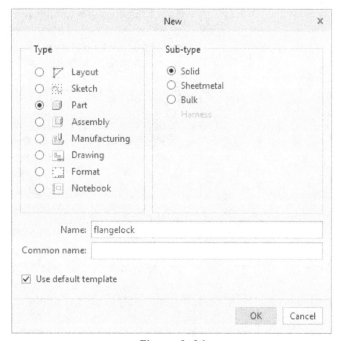

Figure 3–34

- One of the best ways to ensure consistency and compliance with your company's MBD standards is to put as much information into the starts parts as possible. This start part must adhere to the Model Organizational Schema established by your company.

- The required parameter set can be added to the start parts, as well as the layers, layer rules, orientation names and so on.

- You can also set the Detail options to be used for the models by setting them in the start part.

Practice 3a

Create a Start Part

Practice Objectives

- Create a start part and add required parameters.
- Create layers and combination states and then assign Detail options.

To maintain standards and ensure model completeness, models should always begin with a start part. For the purposes of this practice, and for practices going forward, you will work from a simplified MBD Schema. Your company will have its own, far more complete schema, which you will follow in production.

For this schema, you will apply the following to the start part:

Layers and Combination States	• D0_Model_Only
	• D0_Default
	• D1_Site_Map
	• D2_Titles
	• D3_Properties
	• D5_Datums
Parameters	• DESCRIPTION
	• PART_NUMBER
	• MODELED_BY
	• MODELED_DATE
	• REV
	• CAGE_CODE
	• DISTRIBUTION_LEVEL
	• COMPLETENESS_STATE

Task 1 - Create a new model to be the base start part.

1. If required, click 🔄 (Select Working Directory, navigate to the *Creo Parametric Model Based Definition Practice Files* folder and click **OK**.

2. In the Quick Access toolbar, click ▯ (New).

3. In the New dialog box, type **MBD_Start_Part** for the name and remove the checkmark next to **Use default template**.

4. Click **OK**.

5. In the New File Options dialog box, click **Browse**.

6. In the Choose Template dialog box, if the current working directory does not display, click **Working Directory** in the *Common Folders* area.

7. Double-click **metric_start_part.prt**.

8. Note that the **MODELED_BY** and **DESCRIPTION** parameters are already created. Leave them blank, as shown in Figure 3–35.

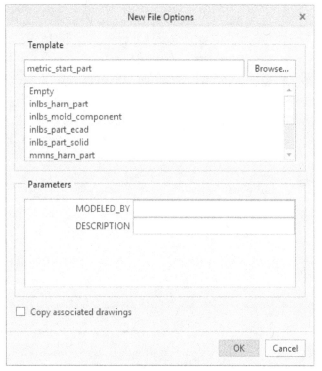

Figure 3–35

9. Click **OK**.

10. In the In-graphics toolbar, apply the following initial setup:

- *(Datum Display Filters):* Enable All

- *(Display Style):* (Shading With Edges)

- *(Spin Center):* Disabled

Task 2 - Add required parameters to the start part.

1. Select the *Tools* tab.

2. Click [ ] (Parameters) to open the Parameters dialog box.

3. Click ✚ (Add New Parameter).

4. Enter **PART_NUMBER** for the parameter name and select **String** from the Type drop-down list, as shown in Figure 3–36.

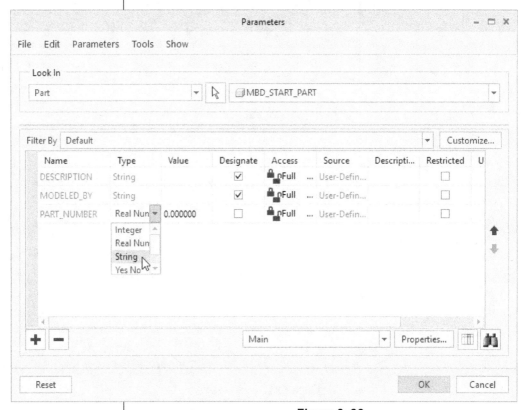

Figure 3–36

5. Enable **Designate** for the new parameter.

6. Repeat the previous steps for the parameters **REV**, **MODELED_DATE**, **DISTRIBUTION_LEVEL**, **COMPLETENESS_STATE**, and **CAGE_CODE,** with Type set to String and the Designate option selected, as shown in Figure 3–37.

Name	Type	Value	Designate	Access	Source	Descripti...	Rest
DESCRIPTION	String		✓	🔒 nFull ...	User-Defin...		[
MODELED_BY	String		✓	🔒 nFull ...	User-Defin...		[
PART_NUMBER	String		✓	🔒 nFull ...	User-Defin...		[
REV	String		✓	🔒 nFull ...	User-Defin...		[
MODELED_DATE	String		✓	🔒 nFull ...	User-Defin...		[
DISTRIBUTION_LEVEL	String		✓	🔒 nFull ...	User-Defin...		[
COMPLETENESS_STATE	String		✓	🔒 nFull ...	User-Defin...		[
CAGE_CODE	String		✓	🔒 nFull ...	User-Defin...		[

Figure 3–37

7. Click **OK**.

Task 3 - Add a relation to control the distribution level note.

1. In the *Tools* tab, click ᵈ= (Relations).

2. In the Relations dialog box, click **File>Import Relations**.

3. Double-click on **distribution_notes.txt**. The relations are imported as shown in Figure 3–38.

The relations are designed to look at the DISTRIBUTION_LEVEL parameter. If it is not A, B, or C the note will indicate that it needs to be set. If it is set to A, B or C then the note will correspond to that distribution level.

Note: *The notes used are illustrative only, and are non-standard. Your company will determine exactly what levels and notes are to be used.*

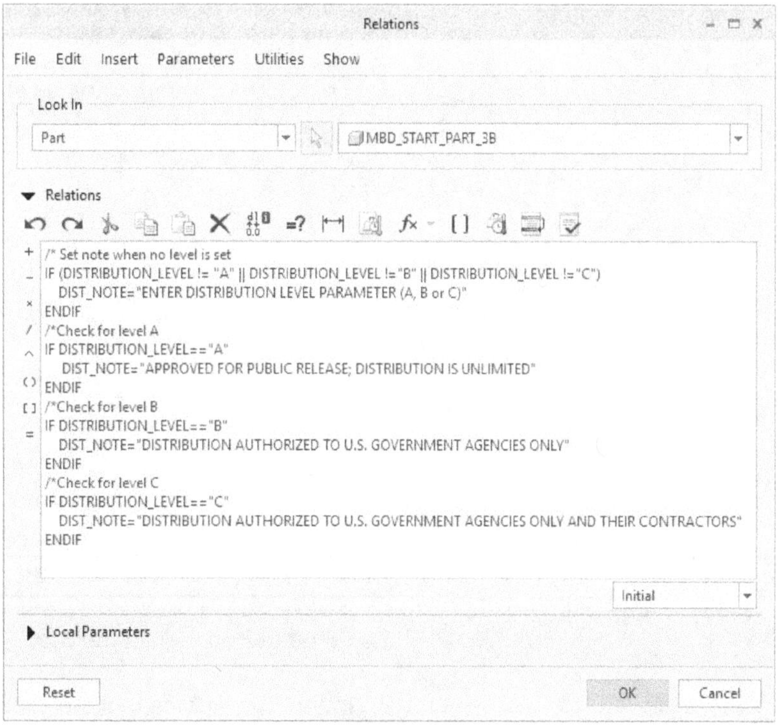

Figure 3–38

4. Click **OK**. The notes will be added in an upcoming task.

Task 4 - Create an empty annotation feature for each combination state.

Design Considerations

It is recommended that annotations be placed into Annotation features. This provides a method for organizing the annotations. To that end, create an annotation feature in the start part for each combination state.

1. Select the *Annotate* tab.

2. In the Annotation Features group of the ribbon, click ⬚⁊ (Annotation Feature).

3. Select the *Properties* tab and type **D0_Default**.

4. Click **OK** and the annotation feature is added to the Model Tree.

When a part is created using this start part, users will simply edit the definition of these annotation features when adding annotations.

5. Repeat the preceding steps to create annotation features named **D1_Site_Map**, **D2_Titles**, **D3_Properties**, and **D5_Datums**.

6. Select all five annotation features in the Model Tree, right-click, and select **Move to footer**.

7. The Model Tree updates as shown in Figure 3–39.

Figure 3–39

Task 5 - Create a set of default combination states.

1. In the ribbon, select the *Model* tab.

2. In the In-graphics toolbar, click 🔲 (View Manager).

3. Select the *All* tab.

4. Click **New** and set the *Name* to **D0_Model_Only**.

5. In the New Presentation State dialog box, click **Reference Originals**.

6. Repeat the previous two steps for combination states named **D0_Default, D1_Site_Map, D2_Titles, D3_Properties**, and **D5_Datums**.

7. Right-click on **D0_Default** and select **Make Default**. This ensures that the model always opens to this combination state.

Note that some companies use Default All in lieu of D0_Default.

8. If required, remove the checkmark in the *Tab Display and Publish* columns next to **Default All**.

If you are in the Annotate tab when you open the view Manager, the Display combined views option will be unavailable to change.

9. Enable **Display combined views**, as shown in Figure 3–40.

Figure 3–40

10. Click **Close** to close the View Manager dialog box.

11. The system displays the combination states at the bottom of the screen, as shown in Figure 3–41.

Figure 3–41

Task 6 - Add a .DTL file to the model.

1. Click **File>Prepare>Model Properties**.

2. In the **Model Properties** dialog box, click **change** in the Detail Options row (you might have to scroll down to see it).

3. Click 📂 (Open Configuration) and double-click on **mm_for_3d.dtl**.

4. Click **OK** in the Options dialog box.

5. Click **Close** to close the Model Properties dialog box.

Task 7 - Add two notes to the D0_Default combination state.

1. Select the *D0_Default* combination state tab.

2. In the ribbon, select the *Annotate* tab.

Notes are covered in detail in another section.

3. In the Model Tree, expand the Footer, select the **D0_Default** annotation feature and select 🖌 (Edit Definition) in the mini toolbar, as shown in Figure 3–42.

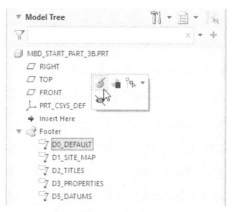

Figure 3–42

4. In the Annotation Planes group, click 🖐 (FLAT TO SCREEN).

5. In the Annotation Feature dialog box, click ᴬ≡ (Note).

6. To place the note, select the location shown in Figure 3–43.

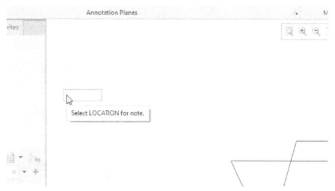

Figure 3–43

7. In the Text group, click (Note From File).

8. Double-click on **security.txt**. The note displays as shown in Figure 3–44.

The note uses the DISTRIBUTION_LEVEL and DIST_NOTE parameters to determine which note to create. Per the relations, since the DISTRIBUTION_LEVEL parameter has not been assigned, the default note is created.

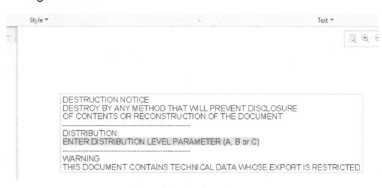

Figure 3–44

9. Click on the screen to complete the note.

10. In the Annotation Feature dialog box, click (Note).

11. To place the note, select the location shown in Figure 3–45.

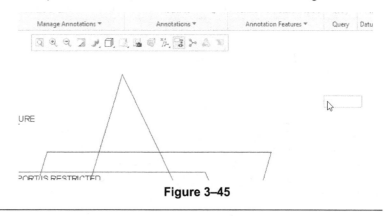

Figure 3–45

12. Type **STATE: &completeness_state** to use the completeness status parameter.

13. Click on the screen to complete the note. The state value will be established when you create a part using the start part and enter a value for the parameter.

14. In the Annotation Feature dialog box, click **OK**.

15. Save the model.

16. Close the window and erase the file.

Design Considerations

More information can be placed into the start part, but tools not yet covered are required. For the purposes of this training, the additional items will be manually added to the models.

Practice 3b

Create a New Model

Practice Objectives

- Create a new model using the start part you created and some basic geometry.
- Ensure the .DTL file is correct and investigate the combination states.

In this practice, you will use the start part you created to generate a new model.

Task 1 - Create a new model.

1. If required, click  (Select Working Directory), navigate to the practice files folder and click **OK**.

2. In the Quick Access toolbar, click ☐ (New).

3. In the New dialog box, set the *Name* to **MBD_Test** and remove the check next to **Use default template**.

4. Click **OK**.

5. In the New File Options dialog box, click **Browse** and double-click on **mbd_start_part_3b.prt**.

6. Fill in the parameters, as shown in Figure 3–46.

To ensure the results going forward are correct, you will use a start part that was already created. You can use the start part you created if you choose.

Figure 3–46

7. Click **OK**.

8. In the In-graphics toolbar, apply the following initial setup:

- ⁎ *(Datum Display Filters):* Enable All
- ⬜ *(Display Style):* ⬜ (Shading With Edges)
- ⤙ *(Spin Center):* Disabled

The model displays, as shown in Figure 3–47.

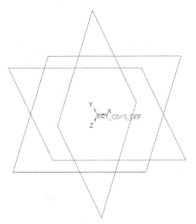

Figure 3–47

Task 2 - Verify that the .DTL has the settings used in the previous practice.

1. Click **File>Prepare>Model Properties**.

2. In the **Model Properties** dialog box, click **change** on the *Detail Options* row.

3. The .DTL file displays in the Options dialog box, as shown in Figure 3–48.

	Value	Default	Status	Description
Active Model				
▼ These options control text not subject to other optio				
text_height	CALCULATED *	calculated	●	Sets the default te
text_thickness	0.000000 *	0.000000	●	Sets default text th
text_width_factor	0.800000 *	0.800000	●	Sets default ratio I
▼ These options control cross sections and their arrow				
show_clipped_annotations	no *	no	●	Determines wheth
▼ These options control dimensions				
ang_unit_trail_zeros	yes *	yes	●	Determines wheth
default_chamf_dim_configuration	leader *	leader	●	Specifies the defa
default_chamf_text_orientation	next_to_and_centered_...	next_to_and_centered_...	●	Defines the defaul
default_diam_dim_arrow_state	inside *	inside	●	Defines the initial
default_chamfer_text	45xd *	45xd	●	Defines the defaul
default_angdim_text_orientation	horizontal *	horizontal	●	Sets the default te
default_cldim_text_orientation	next_to_and_centered_...	next_to_and_centered_...	●	Sets the default te
default_diadim_text_orientation	next_to_and_centered_...	next_to_and_centered_...	●	Sets the default te
default_dim_elbows	yes *	yes	●	Determines wheth
default_lindim_text_orientation	horizontal *	horizontal	●	Sets the default te
default_orddim_text_orientation	parallel_to_and_center...	parallel_to_and_center...	●	Sets the default te
default_raddim_text_orientation	next_to_and_centered_...	next_to_and_centered_...	●	Sets the default te
default_thickness_dim_prefix	NONE *	none	●	Defines the defaul
default_thickness_dim_suffix	THICK *	thick	●	Defines the defaul
default_tolerance_display_style	std_asme *	std_asme	●	Controls the spaci
default_tolerance_mode	nominal *	nominal	●	Sets the default to
dim_text_gap	0.500000 *	0.500000	●	Controls distance

Figure 3–48

4. Click **Close** in the Options dialog box.

5. Click **Close** in the Model Properties dialog box.

Task 3 - Create some simple geometry.

1. In the Model Tree, select datum **RIGHT** and click ⬚ (Extrude) in the mini toolbar.

2. Create the sketch shown in Figure 3–49.

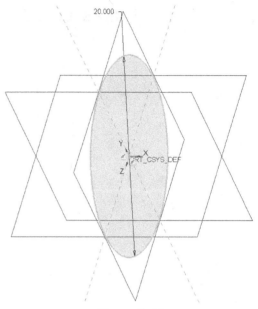

Figure 3–49

3. Click ✔ (OK).

4. Set the *Depth* to **20** and click ✔ (Complete Feature).

5. In the In-graphics toolbar, turn off the display of datum entities.

6. Select the *D0_Default* combination state tab.

7. The basic shape and updated notes display as shown in Figure 3–50.

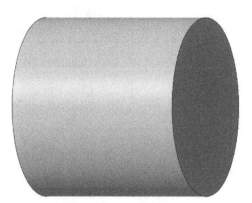

STATE: PRELIMINARY

DESTRUCTION NOTICE
DESTROY BY ANY METHOD THAT WILL PREVENT DISCLOSURE
OF CONTENTS OR RECONSTRUCTION OF THE DOCUMENT

DISTRIBUTION: A
APPROVED FOR PUBLIC RELEASE; DISTRIBUTION IS UNLIMITED

WARNING
THIS DOCUMENT CONTAINS TECHNICAL DATA WHOSE EXPORT IS RESTRICTED

Figure 3–50

Task 4 - Review the combination states brought in by the start part.

1. Select the **Dd0_Model_Only** combination state, and the notes are removed from display as shown in Figure 3–51.

The notes were created in the D0_Default combination state, so are only visible there.

The start part has provided the designer with multiple predefined combination states that will make the job of annotating the model quicker and easier. It also provides consistency as each model will have common states with a common purpose and naming convention.

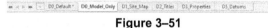

Figure 3–51

2. Save the model.

3. Click **File>Manage Session>Erase Current** and click **Yes**.

Practice 3c

Creating Sections

Practice Objectives

- Create Planar Section in a model.
- Understand the various options in the Section dashboard.

In this practice, you will add two section combination states, then create cross sections for those combination states.

Task 1 - Open a model.

1. If required, click ☑ (Select Working Directory), navigate to the practice files folder and click **OK**.

2. Open **lockinghub_3c.prt**.

3. In the In-graphics toolbar, apply the following initial setup:

- *↗ (Datum Display Filters):* All off

- *▢ (Display Style):* ▢ (Shading With Edges)

- *⊱ (Spin Center):* Disabled

Task 2 - Create the D8_Section_A and D8_Section B combination states.

1. Click the *Annotate* tab.

2. Click through the combination state tabs at the bottom of the window and leave the model on the **D5_Datums** combination state.

3. In the In-graphics toolbar, click ▦ (View Manager).

4. In the View Manager, select the *All* tab.

5. Click **New** and enter **D8_Section_A** as the name.

6. Click **Reference Originals**.

7. Click **New** and enter **D8_Section_B** as the name.

8. Click **Reference Originals**.

9. Double-click on **D8_Section_A** to activate it.

Note that all parts used going forward have the parameters already set. You may change them for example and make yourself the designer, but it is not required to do so.

Task 3 - Create the section that displays the hole details, named section A.

1. Select the *Sections* tab.

2. Expand **New** and select **Y Direction**, as shown in Figure 3–52.

Figure 3–52

3. Type **A** and press <Enter> to set the name. Note that the system automatically selected the **PRT_CSYS_DEF** coordinate system, as shown in Figure 3–53.

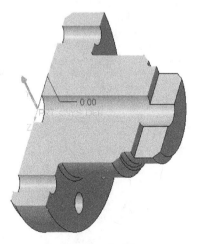

Figure 3–53

This is not the section you want to create, so change the reference axis.

4. Select **X** from the direction drop-down list, as shown in Figure 3–54.

Figure 3–54

5. Drag the arrow to the approximate position, as shown in Figure 3–55.

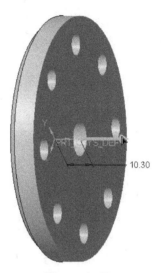

Figure 3–55

6. Click 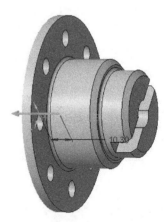 (Flip Clipping Direction) in the dashboard to change the direction, as shown in Figure 3–56.

Figure 3–56

7. Click ✗ (Flip Clipping Direction) to change the direction back.

Task 4 - Investigate additional options in the dashboard.

1. Click ▱ (Cap) to disable it, and spin the model slightly until it displays as shown in Figure 3–57.

The surface capping the section is removed, displaying a surface subset representing the underlying features. This is only a visual representation, and not a shell of the model. The model is still solid.

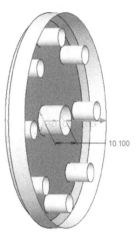

Figure 3–57

2. Click ▱ (Cap) to enable it.

3. Click ▨ (Display Hatch) to display the hatching.

4. Click ⬥ ˅ (Color Palette) to access the color palette.

Remember that at the time of writing, Creo View will only use the model color for sections.

5. Select the color, as shown in Figure 3–58.

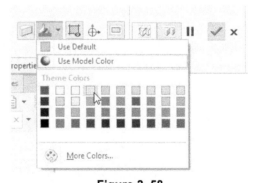

Figure 3–58

6. Click 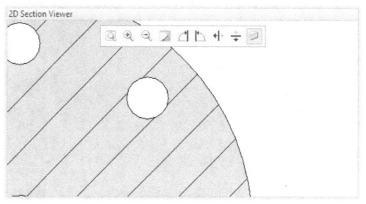 (2D Section View) to view the section in the 2D Section viewer window.

7. Use the middle mouse button to pan and zoom (or use the icons in the 2D Section Viewer to zoom into a section, as shown in Figure 3–59.

Figure 3–59

8. Click (2D Section View) to close the 2D Section viewer window.

Task 5 - Use a datum plane for the section.

1. In the ribbon, expand (Datum) and select ▱ (Plane), as shown in Figure 3–60.

Figure 3–60

2. In the Model Tree, select the hidden plane **RIGHT**.

3. Edit the *Translation* to **10**.

4. Click the *Display* tab and enable **Adjust outline**.

5. Edit the *Width* and *Height* to **100**, as shown in Figure 3–61.

Figure 3–61

6. Select the *Properties* tab and edit the name to **SECTION A**.

7. In the Datum Plane dialog box, click **OK**.

8. In the dashboard, click ▶ (Resume).

9. In the dashboard, change the *Offset* to **Through**.

10. Click ✓ (Apply Changes). The section displays as shown in Figure 3–62.

Figure 3–62

11. In the In-graphics toolbar, expand ⬚ (Saved Orientations) and select **RIGHT**.

12. In the View Manager, select the *Orient* tab.

13. Click **New** and enter **D8_Section_A** for the name.

14. Select the *All* tab.

15. Right-click on **D8_Section_A** and select **Redefine**.

16. Select **D8_Section_A** from the Orientation drop-down list.

17. Select **A** from the Cross section drop-down list.

18. Click **OK**.

Task 6 - Create the D8_Section_B section.

---

1. In the View Manager, double-click on the **D8_Section_B** combination state to activate it.

2. Select the *Sections* tab and click **New>Planar**.

3. Edit the name to **B**.

4. In the ribbon, expand ⬚ (Datum) and select ▱ (Plane).

5. In the Model Tree, select the hidden plane **FRONT**.

6. In the Datum Plane dialog box, change the *Offset* to **Through**.

7. Click the *Display* tab and enable **Adjust outline**.

8. Edit the *Width* and *Height* to **100**.

9. Select the *Properties* tab and edit the name to **SECTION B**.

10. Click **OK** in the Datum Plane dialog box.

11. In the dashboard, click ▶ (Resume).

12. In the dashboard, change the *Offset* to **Through**.

13. Click ⬚ (Display Hatch), and then click ✓ (Apply Changes).

14. In the View Manager, click **Edit>Edit Hatching**.

15. Select aluminum from the list of hatch patterns.

16. Click ⬚ (Halve) for the *Scale*.

17. Select  for the color and click **OK**.

18. In the In-graphics toolbar, expand  (Saved Orientations) and select **FRONT**.

19. In the View Manager, select the *Orient* tab.

20. Click **New** and enter **D8_Section_B** for the name.

21. In the View Manager, select the *All* tab.

22. Right-click on **D8_Section_B** and select **Redefine**.

23. Select **D8_Section_B** from the Orientation drop-down list.

24. Select **B** from the Cross section drop-down list.

25. The D8_SECTION_B dialog box displays as shown in Figure 3–63.

Figure 3–63

26. Click **OK**. The model displays as shown in Figure 3–64.

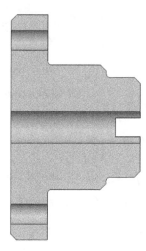

Figure 3–64

27. Select the **D0_Default** combination state.

28. Save the model and erase it from memory.

Chapter Review Questions

1. Configuration options found in **config.pro** are stored in your models.

   a. True

   b. False

2. When adding parameters, you must select the *Type*, which can be:

   a. String

   b. Real Number

   c. Integer

   d. Yes No

   e. All of the above

3. You can control the display of layers in combination states using _____.

   a. Property Display

   b. Layer Groups

   c. Layer States

   d. Simplified Representations

4. Combination states can use different layer states, orientations, appearances, and cross sections to show multiple views of the model.

   a. True

   b. False

5. The combination states displayed at the bottom of the graphics window are predefined by Creo Parametric.

   a. True

   b. False

Answers: 1.b, 2.e, 3.c, 4.a, 5.b

Dimension and Geometric Tolerance Annotations

This chapter introduces how to show and create dimensional annotations, including basic dimensions. In addition, this chapter describes the process used to create datums and geometric tolerances.

Learning Objectives in This Chapter

- Understand the difference between Semantic and Presentation annotations.
- Learn to show and create dimensions and the implications of each practice.
- Create datum references and basic dimensions.
- Create and apply geometric tolerances to the model.

4.1 Semantic and Presentation Annotations

Creo Parametric models are created by adding features that use dimensional parameters. When annotating the model you have two choices. You can show the dimensions that were used to create the model (driving dimensions) or you can create dimensions (driven dimensions) that are driven by the model geometry.

Different companies have different approaches and rules for using shown and created dimensions.

Some advantages of shown or driven dimensions are:

- Easily displayed since they have already been created during the definition of the feature.

- Automatically oriented correctly.

- Organized as elements of the feature to which they belong.

- Known to "fail" only if the feature itself fails.

Semantic annotation is the primary enabler of machine to machine (or software to software) communication. Since shown dimensions for sketched features are related to the sketch dimensions, and not to the surfaces that result from extruding, revolving, or sweeping the section, they do not have a semantic definition by default.

You can make a shown dimension semantic by selecting the annotation and clicking ⊟ (References) in the *Dimension* tab. The References dialog box displays as shown in Figure 4–1, where you can select appropriate geometric references.

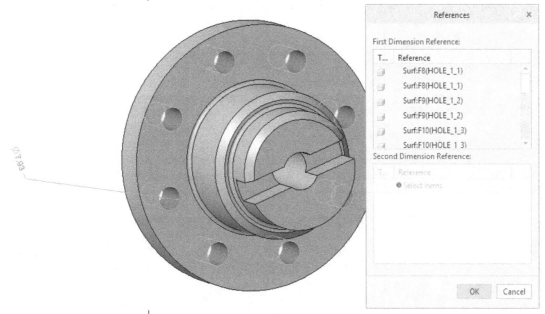

Figure 4–1

Shown dimensions cannot be added to annotation features.

When you create a dimension however, you can do so as part of an Annotation Feature. In the Annotation Feature dialog box, you can select additional surface references to add to the semantic definition using the References collector, as shown in Figure 4–2.

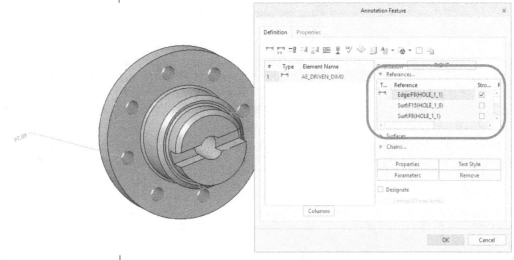

Figure 4–2

4.2 Showing Dimensions

When annotating a model, the dimensions used to create the model can be shown quickly. This process has the advantage of speed, as the dimensions are already created and simply need to be displayed in the appropriate annotation view.

Once dimensions are shown, you can add semantic references, but you cannot add the dimensions to annotation features. Your company will have a standard established for the use of Shown annotations. In this course, you will show and create dimensions so you can handle either scenario.

The first step in any session in which you want to annotate, the model is to activate the appropriate annotation plane. In the *Annotate* tab of the ribbon you have the predefined annotation planes, as shown in Figure 4–3.

Figure 4–3

Once you select the annotation plane, any annotations that are created will be added on that plane. To completely annotate the model, you will use multiple annotation planes. You can change the active annotation plane at any time, but must do so prior to the initialization of the annotation element.

One characteristic of shown dimensions versus created dimensions is that they will be displayed on the plane in which they were created, and are therefore independent of the annotation plane. However, it is recommended to select the annotation plane before showing dimensions, as it might be easier to place dimensions with the model in a planar orientation.

After selecting the appropriate orientation plane, click ⧉ (Active Annotation Plane) to orient the model parallel to the screen.

You can show dimensions using the Show Annotations dialog box, as shown in Figure 4–4.

Until a feature is selected, the Show Annotations dialog box will be empty.

Figure 4–4

The dialog box can be accessed in two ways:

*   In the ribbon, click  (Show Annotations).

*   Select a feature, right-click, and select **Show Annotations**.

When selecting a feature, any dimensions that can be shown will display in red. You can decide which dimensions to retain in your view by clicking them in the graphics window, or selecting them in the Show Annotations dialog box, as shown in Figure 4–5.

Figure 4–5

Any dimensions that are shown will display in the Detail Tree with the preface *DRV* to indicate that they are driving dimensions, as shown in Figure 4–6.

Figure 4–6

In the graphics window, select a dimension and drag it to the appropriate location. Depending on the annotation plane orientation and the way in which the model was dimensioned, you might have to re-orient the dimension text.

*You can change the viewing direction, or use **Text Rotation** to reorient the text.*

In many cases, the text will be oriented incorrectly for the view you are trying to establish. You can right-click on the dimension and select **Change Orientation**. The system will display the grid for the annotation plane, and a blue and red arrow. The red arrow indicate the direction in which the dimension will display, as shown in Figure 4–7.

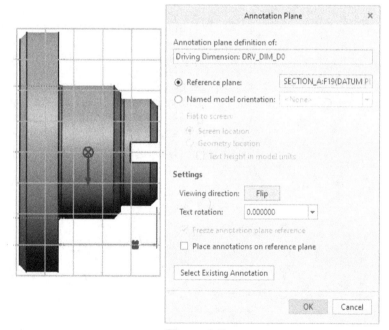

Figure 4–7

By default, shown dimension will display on the plane on which they were created while creating the geometry. Once they have been shown in the model, simply right-click and select **Move to Plane** to move them to a more appropriate plane, if required.

Semantic References

Once a dimension is shown, you can select it on the model or in the Detail Tree, and click **References** in the *Dimension* tab shown in Figure 4–8.

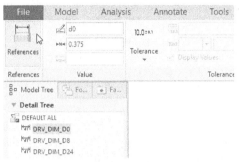

Figure 4–8

The References dialog box opens, where you can add semantic references for the dimension, as shown in Figure 4–9.

Figure 4–9

You can select the **Origin** checkbox to set the witness line as the origin of the dimension. The point of origin displays as a circle at the intersection of the dimension and witness lines. Note that there can only be one origin, so selecting **Origin** for one reference removes it from the other reference.

4.3 Creating Dimensions

When you require dimensional annotations on your model, create the dimensions in the context of an annotation feature. Use the same naming convention for the annotation features as you do for the combination states.

- As with shown dimensions, the first step is to select the appropriate annotation plane from the Annotations Planes group in the ribbon.

- With created dimensions, the annotation plane plays a critical role in how the dimensions display. Dimensions are created on the annotation plane, and the text direction is controlled by the red arrow.

- Always activate the combination state in which you are displaying the annotations prior to creating those annotations. This is important since annotations exist in the combination state in which they are created. They can be added and removed from combination states, but activating the appropriate combination state avoids any additional work.

- Annotation elements shall be oriented in a head on view consistent with the model orientation in which they are created. This is to support the ease of use for non-MBD activities and users. For example, small job shops may still opt to print out the MBD file.

- Although it is recommended to create dimensions inside an annotation feature, you can create dimensions by selecting the applicable icon in the Annotations group of the ribbon, such as ⊢⊣ (Dimension) or ⁼₁₂⁰ (Ordinate Driven Dimension). If you create dimensions outside of an annotation feature, simply select the dimension and click ▽ (Create Annotation Feature) in the mini toolbar.

Standard Dimensions

When you click ⊢⊣ (Dimension), the Select Reference dialog box displays with the available reference selection options, as shown in Figure 4–10.

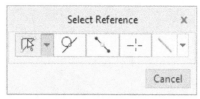

Figure 4–10

The options are described as follows:

Attach Type	Description
⊠ (Entity)	Creates the dimension using the selected reference, such as an edge or point.
⊠ (Surface)	Creates the dimension using the selected surface.
⊠ (Reference)	Create a dimension by selecting any appropriate references.
⊘ (Tangent)	Creates the dimension tangent to an arc or circle.
⟍ (Midpoint)	Creates the dimension using the midpoint of the selected entity.
⊣⊢ (Intersection)	Creates the dimension using the closest intersection point of two selected entities. Press and hold <Ctrl> while selecting each set of intersecting entities.
⟍ (Line)	Creates a two-point line for the dimension reference.
— (Horizontal Line)	Creates a horizontal line for the dimension reference.
│ (Vertical Line)	Creates a vertical line for the dimension reference.

- It is recommended to reference surfaces when creating dimensions, just as when you created the model, since many downstream tools and processes might not recognize or otherwise accept dimensions to edges.

- To create dimension, select the appropriate entities and place the dimension by clicking the middle mouse button.

Ordinate Dimensions

Click $=\!\!\frac{0}{12}$ (Ordinate Driven Dimension) to create ordinate dimensions. Ordinate dimensions are created to establish a set of dimensions from a common dimensioning reference, as shown in Figure 4–11.

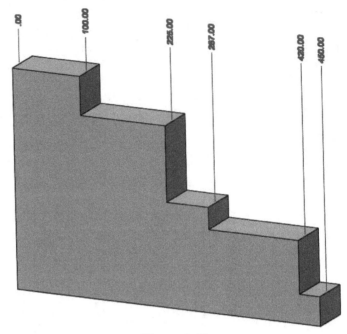

Figure 4–11

- First, select the baseline reference, then select the additional references and click the middle mouse button to place the dimensions.

- The Select References dialog box is also used for Ordinate dimensions, but it only has the 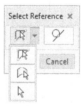 (Entity), (Surface) and (Reference) selection options available, as shown in Figure 4–12.

Figure 4–12

- When creating a set of ordinate dimensions in a model that already contains a baseline, you must first click **Create a New Baseline** or **Select Existing Baseline**, depending on how you need to create your dimensions, as shown in Figure 4–13.

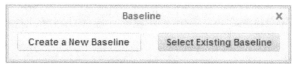

Figure 4–13

- As with shown dimension, click a dimension and drag it to the appropriate location. Re-orient the dimension text, if required, using the right-click on the **Current Orientation** option.

4.4 Datum Feature Symbols

Datum references provide the basis for all geometrical tolerancing in the model. The datum reference, created using the

⏣ (Datum Feature Symbol) option, defines an origin from which the location or geometric characteristics of all of the geometry of a part or assembly model can be established. For example, datums **A** and **B** have been defined for the simple part, as shown in Figure 4–14. The left and bottom sides of the part will be used as an origin to locate the position of the hole using the 0.001 boundary defined by the geometrical tolerance.

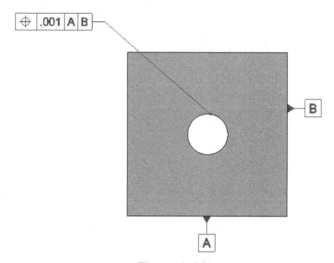

Figure 4–14

The first step is to activate the appropriate combination state and annotation plane.

Set Datum Feature Symbols are created in the context of an annotation feature. Select ▽ (Annotation Feature) from the Annotation Features group in the ribbon, or edit the definition of an existing annotation feature. Then, click ⏣ (Datum Feature Symbol) in the Annotation Feature dialog box and a preview is immediately attached to the cursor. Drag the preview to the attachment reference, then press the middle mouse button to place it, as shown in Figure 4–15.

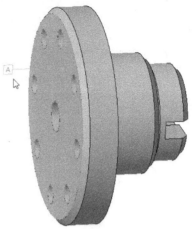

Figure 4–15

The datum feature options are available in the *Datum Feature* tab, as shown in Figure 4–16. This tab displays after the datum is placed on the screen. To close the tab, click anywhere on the screen. If you select a datum from the screen, the tab opens.

Note that you can select the 🔲 (References) option to add additional semantic references to the Datum Feature Symbol.

Figure 4–16

After the annotation feature is complete, move it to the regeneration Footer. You can change the attachment reference by selecting the DFS and clicking 🔗 (Change Reference) in the mini toolbar, as shown in Figure 4–17.

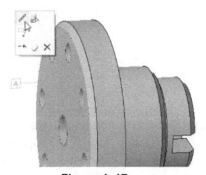

Figure 4–17

Automatic Naming

When you create a datum feature symbol, the next available name in the standard sequence (A, B, C, etc.) is automatically assigned. You can manually enter a label at any time using the field in the *Datum Feature* dashboard. If a datum label in the sequence is missing, the next datum created will have the missing label. For example, if datum A and datum C exist on the drawing, the next label will automatically be assigned to B.

Additional Text

You can include additional text with a datum feature symbol using the *Additional text* field. If you click (Rotate Text Position), the text will move around the datum label, as shown in Figure 4–18.

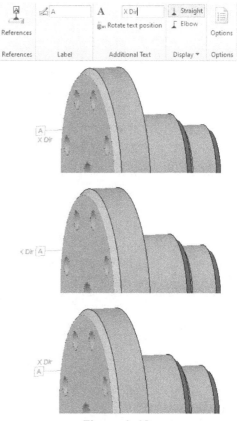

Figure 4–18

Adding Elbows

You can click ⊥ (Elbow) to add an elbow to the datum feature symbol. You can adjust the length of the elbow by pressing <Shift> when you drag the label.

4.5 Converting Legacy Datums

Prior to Creo Parametric 4.0, Set Datums were derived from existing datum planes or axes. Now, Datum Feature Symbols must be associated with model geometry. This means that when you open a model that was created in Creo Parametric 3.0 or earlier, you have to update any existing Set Datums to Datum Feature Symbols if you need to make any changes to dimensions, Geometric Tolerances, and so on. It is important to note that the Set Datums might also be connected to geometric tolerances, so you must manage that circumstance as well.

As of Creo Parametric 4.0 M060, a Legacy Datum Annotations Conversion tool is available to help convert legacy datums to Datum Feature Symbol annotations.

The following steps should be followed:

1. Ensure the configuration option **combined_state_type** is set to **semi_mbd**.
2. Right-click an annotation in the Detail Tree or Annotations group in the Model Tree and click **Convert All**, as shown in Figure 4–19.

Figure 4–19

3. In the ribbon, select the *Annotate* tab and click
Annotations>Legacy Datum Annotations Conversion to
open the Legacy Datum Annotations Conversion dialog box,
as shown in Figure 4–20.

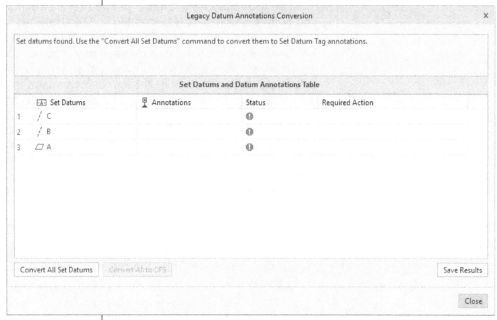

Figure 4–20

Note the following:

- If you are working in Drawing mode, you must open the
  model and access the Legacy Datum Annotations
  Conversion dialog box from there.

- If you are working in Assembly mode, you must access
  the Legacy Datum Annotations Conversion dialog box
  from the top model.

- For annotations assigned from an inheritance feature, the
  Legacy Datum Annotations Conversion dialog box must
  be accessed from the source model.

4. All legacy Set Datums must be converted to Set Datum Tag
annotations. Click **Convert All Set Datums** to complete that
conversion. The results of the conversion appear in the Set
Datums and Datum Annotations Table of the Legacy Datum
Annotations Conversion dialog box, as shown in Figure 4–21.

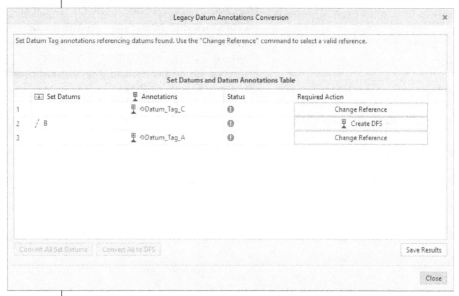

Figure 4–21

- If the conversion is successful, the datum is moved from the Set Datums column to the Annotations column and the Status column is empty.

- When a conflict is encountered, the datum is moved from the Set Datums column to the Annotations column, and 🔴 displays in the Status column. **Change Reference** appears in the Required Actions column.

- When a failure is encountered, the datum stays in the Set Datums column and 🔴 displays in the Status column. **Create DFS** displays in the Required Actions column.

- You can hover over 🔴 to see additional information related to a conflict or failure, as shown in Figure 4–22.

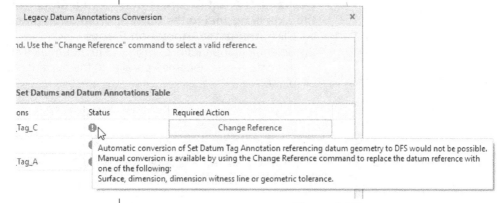

Figure 4–22

5. Resolve the conversion conflicts by clicking **Change Reference** and selecting a reference on the model. The legacy Set Datum Tag annotation converts to a Datum Feature Symbol annotation. This must be repeated for all conflicts. Once corrected, the Annotations turn green, as shown in Figure 4–23.

Figure 4–23

6. When Creo Parametric cannot convert a legacy Set Datum, **Create DFS** displays in the Required Action column, indicating a failure. Review each failure and match it to one of the following scenarios. Use the indicated steps to correct it.

Scenario 1: A Set Datum is placed on a datum axis and the axis is normal to the current orientation plane.
1. Click **Annotate>Annotation Planes**.
2. Select a plane that is parallel to the datum axis such that the datum axis becomes parallel to the current orientation plane.

Scenario 2: A Set Datum is placed on a datum axis and the axis is at an angle to the current orientation plane.

1. Create a datum plane passing through the datum axis.
2. Click **Annotate>Annotation Planes** and select the new datum plane.
3. Click **Active Annotation Plane** so that the datum axis becomes parallel to the current orientation plane.

Scenario 3: A model Set Datum is placed on a Geometric Tolerance that was created in Drawing mode with the As Free Note placement type.

Since the Geometric Tolerance was created as a free note in Drawing mode, it fails to convert because it does not have any reference in the model and is treated as a draft Geometric Tolerance in Part mode.

1. In the Drawing Tree or the Model Tree, select the draft Geometric Tolerance and click ⚲ (Edit References) from the mini toolbar.
2. Select the appropriate reference on the model.

Scenario 4: A model Set Datum is placed on a model Geometric Tolerance that was placed on a model dimension in Drawing mode. The dimension was created with the Dimension Elbow placement type and an Edge reference.

The Geometric Tolerance fails to convert because it was created with an edge reference in Drawing mode and so does not have any reference in the model. Creo Parametric treats it as a draft Geometric Tolerance in Part mode.

1. In the Model Tree, select the draft Geometric Tolerance and click ⚲ (Edit References) from the mini toolbar.
2. Select an edge on the model to temporarily place the Geometric Tolerance.
3. Again, select the Geometric Tolerance and click ⚲ (Edit References) from the mini toolbar.
4. Select the dimension on which to place the Geometric Tolerance.
5. Right-click the Geometric Tolerance and select **Dimension Elbow**.

Scenario 5: A model Set Datum is placed on a model Geometric Tolerance that was placed on a model leader note in Drawing mode. The note was placed with the Note Elbow placement type.

The Geometric Tolerance fails to convert because it was created with a model leader note in Drawing mode and so does not have any reference in the model. Creo Parametric treats it as a draft Geometric Tolerance in Part mode.

1. In the Model Tree, select the draft Geometric Tolerance and click ✐ (Edit References) from the mini toolbar.
2. Select the leader note as a reference on the model.

7. Repeat Step 6 for all of the failures that have a workaround, then click **Convert All Set Datums** to convert the legacy Set Datums to Set Datum Tag annotations.
8. If no workaround (from Step 6) is available for the failure, click **Create DFS** to create a new Datum Feature Symbol annotation. The Datum Feature Symbol annotation appears in green with the same name as the set datum. Repeat this step for all failures that do not otherwise have a workaround. Once complete, the Annotations display in green as shown in Figure 4–24.

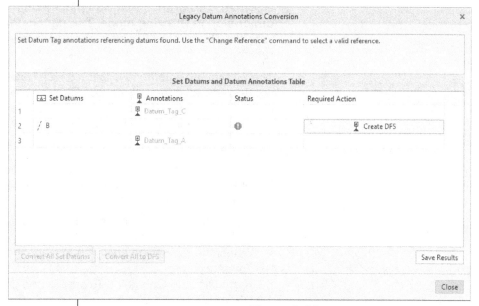

Figure 4–24

9. If any legacy Set Datum Tag annotations remain, click **Convert All to DFS** to convert all of them to Datum Feature Symbol annotations, which will appear in green.

Note that you can use the **Save Results** option to save the current state of Set Datums and the Datum Annotations Table to an information file.

If you are working in a drawing, you have to open the part to perform the conversion operations. Once you have finished, return to the drawing and update all sheets using the following steps:

1. If there are multiple sheets, right-click a sheet and click **Select All**.
2. Select the *Review* tab and click **Update Sheets** from the **Update** group. This will update all of the drawing sheets.
3. Select the *Annotate* tab and click (Show Model Annotations) to display the new Datum Feature Symbols.

4.6 Geometric Tolerances

Specifying geometric tolerances in Creo Parametric enables you to set critical surfaces, explain how they relate to one another, and set inspection criteria. Unlike dimensional tolerances, geometric tolerances do not have an effect on geometry.

Geometric Tolerances can be added to the model either as stand alone annotation elements or as part of an annotation feature. As with all other annotations, you should first set the annotation plane.

How To: Create a Geometric Tolerance

1. Select the *Annotate* tab to activate the annotation options.
2. Select the combination state to which you want to add the Geometric Tolerance.
3. In the Annotation Features group, click ⊐⎮ (Annotation Feature) or edit the definition of an existing annotation feature.
4. In the Annotation Feature dialog box, click ⊡⎮⎮ (Geometric Tolerance) to start the creation of a geometric tolerance.
5. Select the entity to which you want to attach the geometric tolerance. The geometric tolerance will display as shown in Figure 4–25.

Figure 4–25

6. The *Geometric Tolerance* tab in the ribbon displays as shown in Figure 4–26.

Figure 4–26

7. If attaching the geometric tolerance with a leader, move the geometric tolerance to the required position and click the middle mouse button to place the geometric tolerance.

8. Select the type of geometric tolerance by choosing an option from the **Geometric Characteristic** menu, as shown in Figure 4–27.

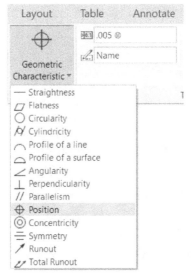

Figure 4–27

9. In the Tolerance & Datum group, enter a value for the tolerance, as show in Figure 4–28.

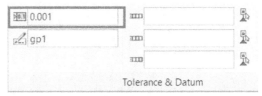

Figure 4–28

10. In the Tolerance & Datum group, enter a value for the tolerance *Name*, as show in Figure 4–29.

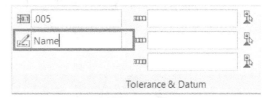

Figure 4–29

11. Set the Datums to be referenced in the Geometric Tolerance. You can select an existing Datum Feature Symbol from the drawing by first selecting ⊥ (Datum Reference) in the Tolerance & Datum group, next to the *Primary*, *Secondary*, or *Tertiary* datum fields, as shown in Figure 4–30.

Figure 4–30

You may also type in the Datum Reference fields instead of selecting a datum from the drawing.

If you type the name of a datum that is already in the model or drawing, it will display in green text in the dashboard. If not, it will display in black text indicating the datum has yet to be defined.

12. Select the datum feature symbol (in this case Datum A) from the drawing as the Primary datum reference. The GTOL updates as shown in Figure 4–31.

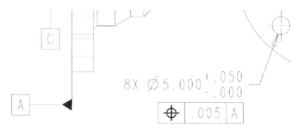

Figure 4–31

13. Select the Secondary and Tertiary datums, as required. The geometric tolerance updates as shown in Figure 4–32, with datum C selected as the Secondary datum reference.

Figure 4–32

14. Additional symbols may now be added to the geometric tolerance. First, click in the field in which you want to add the text or symbol. Then, add a maximum material condition symbol after the tolerance value, as shown in Figure 4–33.

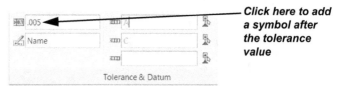

Figure 4–33

You can type spaces as required, to separate symbols and text.

15. In the *Geometric Tolerance* tab, expand  (Symbols) and select a symbol, as shown in Figure 4–34.

Figure 4–34

- The geometric tolerance updates to show the maximum material condition symbol, as shown in Figure 4–35.

Figure 4–35

- You can add additional symbols in other locations, such as maximum material condition after datum C, as shown in Figure 4–36.

Figure 4–36

16. Additional text may also be added above, below, to the left or to the right of the geometric tolerance. Enter text in the appropriate filed in the Additional Text panel, as shown in Figure 4–37.

Figure 4–37

Symbols may also be included in the additional text fields.

The geometric tolerance updates with the additional text, as shown in Figure 4–38.

Figure 4–38

17. Once the geometric tolerance is complete, click on the screen.

18. Once the geometric tolerance is created, you must select all of the surfaces to which the geometric tolerance applies. Press <Ctrl> and select the surfaces, which are then added to the References list, as shown in Figure 4–39.

Figure 4–39

19. Click **OK** to complete the annotation feature.
20. Move the annotation feature to the regeneration Footer in the Model Tree.

A Note on Selection

By default, you are placed in the **References** collector in the Annotation Feature dialog box. Using this collector, you can select individual edges and surfaces. If you want to use more advanced selection techniques, such as **Seed and Boundary** or **Loop** surfaces, expand the **Surfaces** collector, as shown in Figure 4–40.

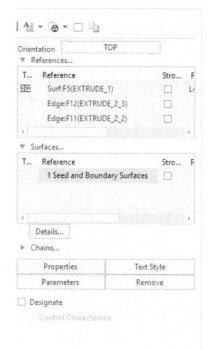

Figure 4–40

While in this collector, you can select individual, seed and boundary, and loop surfaces. You can also click **Details** to open the Surface Sets dialog box, as shown in Figure 4–41.

Figure 4–41

Here, you can add surface sets as well as exclude surfaces from selection.

Composite Geometric Tolerances

You can create composite tolerance frames by clicking

⊞ (Composite Frame) in the *Geometric Tolerance* dashboard. The Composite Frame panel that expands enables you to edit the tolerances and datums, as shown in Figure 4–42.

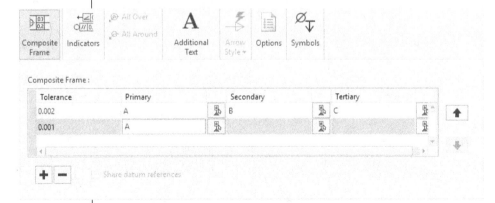

Figure 4–42

ISO GPS Indicators

You can click ⌀╫ (Indicators) in the *Geometric Tolerance* dashboard to add indicators to your Geometric Tolerance to comply with ISO GPS standards. You can click ⌀╫ (Indicators) to expand the *Indicators Frame*, as shown in Figure 4–43.

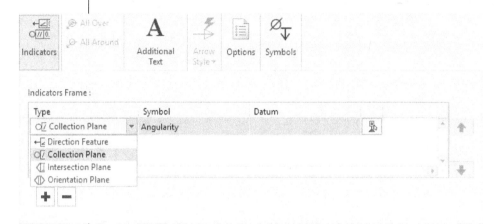

Figure 4–43

4.7 Syntax Checking

Datum target and Geometric tolerance annotations have built-in syntax checking. This ensures that the following comply with ASME and ISO GD&T standards:

- Datum names.

- The datum reference for Datum targets.

- The specified tolerance value and datum references, including modifiers, for Geometric tolerances.

Datum and Datum Target

When working with datum feature symbols, if you enter a value for the datum label that does not comply with standards, you will receive a notification. The datum labels are checked to ensure that they conform to the conventions specified by the ASME Y14.5 standard. To comply with the standard, the label must be either one or two uppercase letters, where the letters O, Q, and I are not permitted. In the example shown in Figure 4–44, the datum name was entered in lowercase, which does not meet the standard requirement that it should be uppercase. The system highlights it in the dashboard as well as on the drawing.

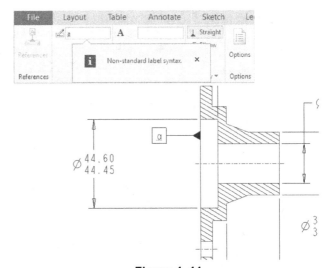

Figure 4–44

Datum features follow the convention of a letter proceeded by a number. For datum targets, if the text typed into the datum reference field does not meet the standard convention, it is identified in the ribbon as well as in the graphics area, as shown in Figure 4–45.

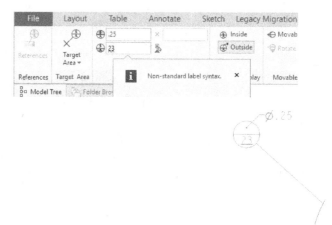

Figure 4–45

In either case, fixing the datum feature reference to comply with the convention clears the syntax check error.

Geometric Tolerance

When working with geometric tolerance annotations, if the text or symbols entered in the value or datum reference fields do not meet the standard, the issue is highlighted in the *Geometric Tolerance* tab and the graphics area, as shown in Figure 4–46.

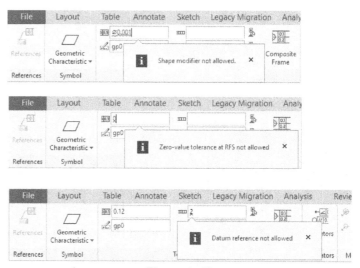

Figure 4–46

4.8 Semantic Query

The Semantic Query option presents semantic information related to annotations. In the Query group in the *Annotate* tab, click ⛏ (Semantic Query) and the Semantic Query toolbar opens, as shown in Figure 4–47.

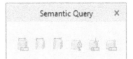

Figure 4–47

The options in the Semantic Query toolbar are grayed out until an annotation is selected. You can query annotations and analyze the relationships between them and the geometry in the Model-Based Definition environment.

The options in the Semantic Query toolbar display or hide related semantic options, as described in the following table:

Option	Description
🔲 (Similar)	Displays all the annotations describing the highlighted references of the currently selected annotation.
📄 (Primary References)	Displays the primary references of the selected annotation.
📄 (Secondary References)	Displays the references of annotations associated with the currently selected annotation (secondary references).
📄 (Associated Datum Symbols)	Displays the datum symbols, such as Datum Feature and Datum Target, associated with the currently selected annotation.
📐 (Associated DRF)	Displays a Datum Reference Frame (DRF) coordinate system associated with the currently selected GTOL.
📐 (Associated GTOLs)	Displays a GTOL associated with the currently selected datum symbol, such as Datum Feature or Datum Target.

When you select an object, it is highlighted in a different color. The colors for **Primary**, **Secondary**, **Preselection**, and **Selected** highlighting can be customized.

4.9 Basic Dimensions

A Basic dimension is a theoretically exact dimension, and is identified with a box around it, as shown in Figure 4–48.

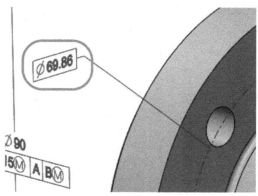

Figure 4–48

You can identify dimensions as basic by selecting the dimension, expanding **Tolerance** and selecting **Basic**, as shown in Figure 4–49.

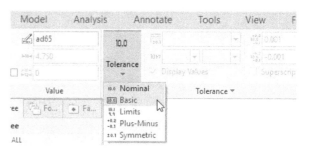

Figure 4–49

Practice 4a

Dimensions and Tolerances

Practice Objective

- Add annotations to the model, including dimensions and tolerances.

In this practice, you will add annotations to the Locking Hub model. Adding dimensions and tolerances to the model should be the first step in any annotation activity for a model, as it enables you to specify material conditions for the geometric tolerances.

Task 1 - Open the part file.

1. If required, click ⌷ (Select Working Directory), navigate to the practice files folder, and click **OK**.

2. Open **lockinghub_4a.prt**.

3. In the In-graphics toolbar, apply the following initial setup:

   - ˣ⁄⁎ *(Datum Display Filters):* All off

   - ⌷ *(Display Style):* ⌷ (Shading With Edges)

   - ⌷ *(Annotation Display):* Enabled

   - ⌷ *(Spin Center):* Disabled

Task 2 - Enable the display of tolerances and set the tolerancing standard.

Design Considerations

Before you begin the creation of any tolerances and annotations, ensure that the correct tolerancing standard has been defined and that the tolerance display is enabled. As annotations are created, they use the standard that has been set. Although this standard can be changed after annotations are created, it is best to ensure the correct standard before creating any annotation.Your company certainly has a standard configuration file that sets theses options for you, but for the purposes of this course, you will set them manually.

1. Select **File>Options** to open the Creo Parametric Options dialog box.

2. Select **Configuration Editor** and click **Find**.

3. Set the *Type keyword* field to **tol_display** and press <Enter>.

4. Set the *Set value* to **Yes**, if required. If so, click **Add / Change** to save the changes.

5. Type **tolerance_standard** in the *Type keyword* field and press Enter.

6. Change the *Set value* to **ansi***, if required. If so, click **Add / Change** to save the changes.

7. Close the Find Options dialog box and click **OK**.

8. In the Creo Parametric Options confirmation dialog box, click **No**, as shown Figure 4–50.

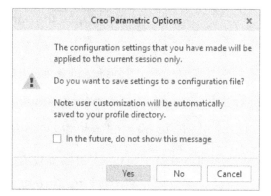

Figure 4–50

Task 3 - Review the predefined annotation planes.

1. Select the *Annotate* tab in the ribbon.

2. Select the **D3_Properties** Combination State at the bottom of the graphics window.

3. In the Annotation Planes group in the ribbon, click (FRONT) then (Active Annotation Plane), and the model orients, as shown in Figure 4–51.

4. In the Annotation Planes group in the ribbon, click ◢ (RIGHT) then ⚏ (Active Annotation Plane), and the model orients, as shown in Figure 4–52.

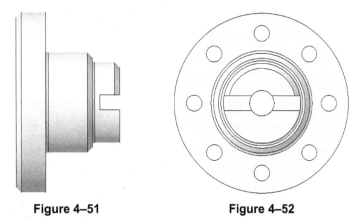

Figure 4–51   **Figure 4–52**

Task 4 - Create a set of overall dimensions in the D3_Properties combination state.

1. Orient the model approximately as shown in Figure 4–53.

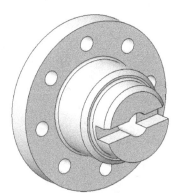

Figure 4–53

2. Select the ◢ (RIGHT) annotation plane.

3. Expand the **Footer** node in the Model Tree.

4. Select **D3_PROPERTIES** in the Footer and click ✎ (Edit Definition).

5. In the Annotation Feature dialog box, click ⊢⊣ (Reference Dimension).

6. In the Select Reference dialog box, select 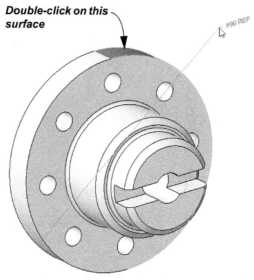 (Surface), if required.

7. Double-click on the outer surface of the flange and move the cursor to the location shown in Figure 4–54.

Double-click on this surface

ø90 REF

Figure 4–54

8. Click the middle mouse button to place the dimension.

9. In the Display group in the ribbon, click 1⊢ (Display) and click **Flip** for the arrow direction, as shown in Figure 4–55.

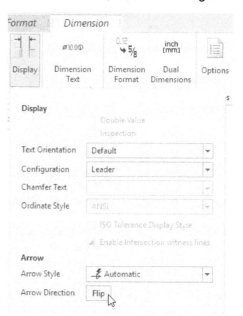

Figure 4–55

10. Press the middle mouse button to complete the dimension placement.

Creo Parametric treats the cylindrical surface as two halves, so each half must be selected.

11. In the Annotation Feature dialog box, in the *References* field, select the other half of the cylindrical flange.

12. Select the ☁ (FRONT) annotation plane.

13. In the Annotation Feature dialog box, click ⟷ (Reference Dimension).

14. Press and hold <Ctrl> and select the two surfaces shown in Figure 4–56.

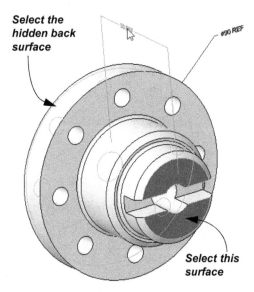

Figure 4–56

15. Click the middle mouse button to place the dimension.

16. Press the middle mouse button a second time to complete the placement.

17. Click **OK** to complete the annotation feature.

18. Select the linear dimension, right-click, and select **Move to Plane**.

19. In the Model Tree, select **FRONT**.

20. In the In-graphics toolbar, select 🗔 (View Manager).

21. In the View Manager, select the *Orient* tab.

22. Click **New** and edit the name to **D3_Properties**.

23. Select the *All* tab.

24. Right-click on **D3_Properties** and select **Redefine**.

25. Select **D3_Properties** from the Orientation drop-down list. The D3_PROPERTIES dialog box updates as shown in Figure 4–57.

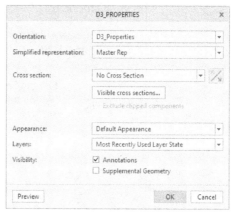

Figure 4–57

26. Click **OK**.

27. Select **File>Options** to open the Creo Parametric Options dialog box.

28. Select **Configuration Editor** and click **Find**.

29. Set the *Type keyword* field to **parenth** and press <Enter>.

30. Select **parenthesize_ref_dim**.

31. Set the *Set value* to **Yes**, if required. If so, click **Add / Change** to save the changes.

32. Close the Find Options dialog box and click **OK**.

33. In the Creo Parametric Options confirmation dialog box, click **No**.

34. Move any dimensions required to clean up the dimension locations, so the model displays as shown in Figure 4–58.

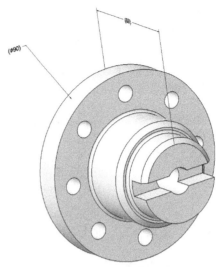

Figure 4–58

35. Click **Close** in the View Manager.

36. Click the *D3_Properties* tab to clear the section display.

Task 5 - Create an annotation feature to add a reference dimension to the D8_Section_A combination state.

---

1. Select the **D8_Section_A** combination state.

2. In the Model Tree, expand **Pattern 1 of Hole 1**, right-click the first instance, and select **Information>Feature Information**.

3. The embedded browser open to display the feature information. Note that the *Relations* area there is a relation driving the angle dimension (**D17**) between features, as shown in Figure 4–59. The dimension **p19** is the number of holes in the pattern.

MAIN PATTERN DIMENSIONS:

Dimension ID	▽	Dimension Value	▽	Displayed Value	▽
d12		7.93 (0.01, -0.01)		7.93 Dia	
d16		69.36 (0.01, -0.01)		69.36 Dia	
d17		45.0 (0.5, -0.5)		45	
d18		45.0 (0.5, -0.5)		45	

Relation Table		
Relation	Parameter	New Value
	Part relations driven by this feature:	
d17 =360/p19	D17	4.500000e+01

Figure 4–59

4. Close the browser panel.

5. Select the ◀ (RIGHT) annotation plane.

The D8_Section_A combination state was not in the start part, so an annotation feature does not yet exist for it.

6. In the Annotation Features group in the ribbon, click ⌐7 (Annotation Feature).

7. In the Annotation Feature dialog box, click ↤→ (Reference Dimension).

8. In the Select Reference dialog box, select ⌐↘ (Surface) from the Selection drop-down list.

9. Spin the model slightly and double-click on the surface shown in Figure 4–60 and move the cursor to the position shown.

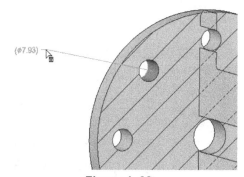

Figure 4–60

10. Click the middle mouse button to place the dimension.

11. In the Dimension Text group in the ribbon, click ⌀10⌀ (Dimension Text).

12. Type a space after the @D text then type **DRILL - &P19 HOLES**, as shown in Figure 4–61.

Figure 4–61

13. In the ribbon, click ↑↑ (Display).

14. Click **Flip** to change to a single arrow.

15. Press the middle mouse button to complete the dimension.

16. In the Annotation Feature dialog box, select the *Properties* tab.

17. Edit the annotation feature Name to **D8_Section_A**.

Design Considerations

At this point, you must select all of the surfaces to which this dimension applies, which is all internal surfaces of the hole pattern.

18. In the Annotation Feature dialog box, select the *Definition* tab.

19. Select **Surface** from the selection filter in the lower right of the Creo Parametric window.

20. Press and hold <Ctrl> and select all of the inside surfaces, as shown in Figure 4–62. Remember to select both halves of each hole.

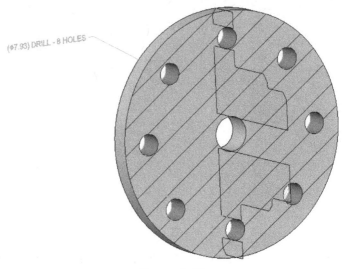

Figure 4–62

21. In the Annotation Feature dialog box, click **OK**.

22. Select the dimension text, right-click and select **Move to Plane**.

23. Select the **SECTION_A** datum plane.

24. Select the *D8_Section_A* combination state tab. The model displays as shown in Figure 4–63.

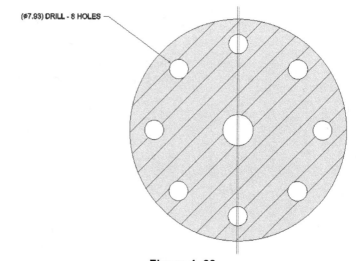

Figure 4–63

25. In the Model Tree, right-click the **D8_SECTION_A** annotation feature and select **Move to footer**.

26. Click through the various Combination States and note that the dimension only displays in the **D8_Section_A** combination state.

Task 6 - Add a Datum Feature Symbol and several dimensions to the D5_Datums annotation feature.

---

1. Select the **D5_Datums** combination state.

2. In the Footer node of the Model Tree, select the **D5_Datums** combination state and click 🖌 (Edit Definition).

3. Select the ⬦ (FRONT) annotation plane.

4. In the Annotation Feature dialog box, click ⬚ (Datum Feature Symbol).

5. Select the surface of flange of the model and move the cursor to the position shown in Figure 4–64.

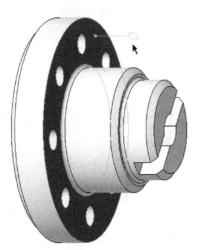

Figure 4–64

6. Press the middle mouse button to place the Datum Feature Symbol, and note that it is automatically named **A**, as shown in Figure 4–65.

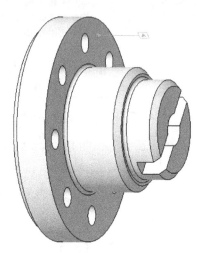

Figure 4–65

7. Click on the screen to complete the datum placement.

8. Select the *Definition* tab.

9. Reorient the model approximately as shown in Figure 4–66.

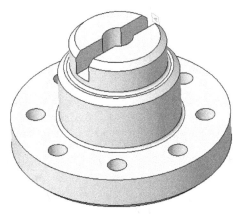

Figure 4–66

10. Right-click on the Datum Feature Symbol and select **Properties**.

11. Drag the location to the position shown in Figure 4–67.

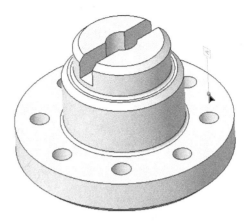

Figure 4–67

12. Click on the screen to complete the move.

13. In the Annotation Planes group, click (RIGHT).

14. In the Annotation Feature dialog box, click ↦ (Dimension).

15. Double-click on the surface shown in Figure 4–68.

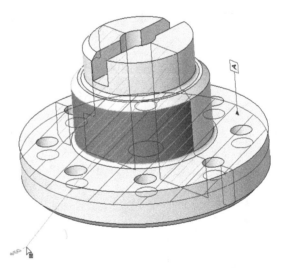

Figure 4–68

16. Press the middle mouse button to place the dimension.

17. In the Display group in the ribbon, click ⇅ (Display) and click **Flip** to flip the arrow direction.

18. In the Tolerances group, expand 10.0 (Tolerance) and select **Symmetric**.

19. In the *Tolerance* field, enter **0.01**. Press the middle mouse button to complete the dimension and the display updates as shown in Figure 4–69.

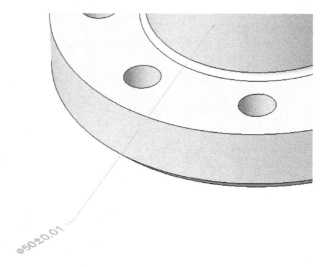

Figure 4–69

20. Click in the references collector and select both sides of the cylindrical surface to which the dimension is attached.

21. In the Annotation Feature dialog box, click ⊢⊣ (Dimension).

22. Double-click on the surface shown in Figure 4–70.

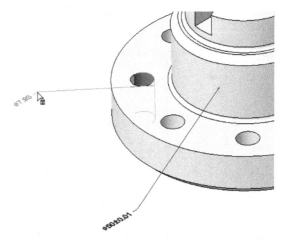

Figure 4–70

23. Press the middle mouse button to place the dimension.

24. In the Display group in the ribbon, click ⁱᶠ (Display) and click **Flip** to flip the arrow direction.

25. In the Tolerances group, expand ¹⁰·⁰ (Tolerance) and select **Symmetric**.

26. In the *Tolerance* field, enter **0.05**. Press the middle mouse button to complete the dimension and the display updates as shown in Figure 4–71.

Figure 4–71

27. Click in the references collector and select both sides of each of the holes in the pattern to which the dimension is attached, as shown in Figure 4–72.

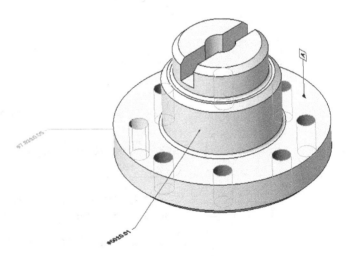

Figure 4–72

28. In the Annotation Feature dialog box, click **OK**.

29. In the In-graphics toolbar, click ▣ (View Manager).

30. Select the *Orient* tab.

31. Click **New** and edit the name to **D5_Datums**.

32. Select the *All* tab.

33. Right-click on **D5_Datums** and select **Redefine**.

34. In the Orientation drop-down list, select **D5_Datums**.

35. In the D5_DATUMS dialog box, click **OK**.

36. Close the View Manager.

37. Select the **7.93** dimension, right-click, and select **Move to Plane**.

38. Select the top surface of the flange and the combination state displays as shown in Figure 4–73.

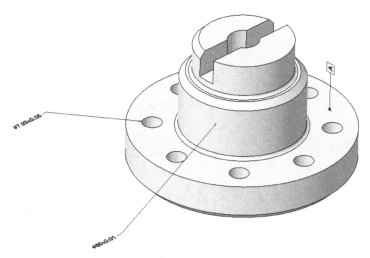

Figure 4–73

Task 7 - Update the dimension for the pattern of holes to add text.

1. Recall from Task 5 that the symbolic name for the number of instances in the hole pattern in **p19**.

2. Select the **7.93** diameter dimension.

3. In the Dimension Text group in the ribbon, click ⌀10◦ (Dimension Text).

4. Edit the text in the *Dimension Text* field, as shown in Figure 4–74.

Figure 4–74

5. Click on the screen to complete the edit.

6. Select the **D0_Default** combination state.

7. Save the model and erase it.

Practice 4b

Geometric Tolerances

Practice Objectives

- Add geometric tolerance annotations, datum annotations, and basic dimension annotations.
- Use the Semantic Query tool.

In this practice, you will create datums, dimensions and geometric tolerances.

Task 1 - Open the part file.

1. If required, click ⬚ (Select Working Directory), navigate to the practice files folder and click **OK**.

2. Open **lockinghub_4b.prt**.

3. In the In-graphics toolbar, apply the following initial setup:

    - ⬚ *(Datum Display Filters):* Enable All

    - ⬚ *(Display Style):* ⬚ (Shading With Edges)

    - ⬚ *(Annotation Display):* Enabled

    - ⬚ *(Spin Center):* Disabled

4. Select the **D5_Datums** combination state, and the model displays as shown in Figure 4–75.

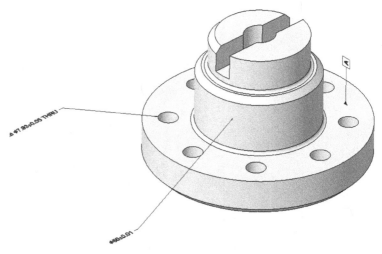

Figure 4–75

Task 2 - Create a geometric tolerance.

1. Select the *Annotate* tab in the ribbon.

2. In the Annotation Planes group in the ribbon, click 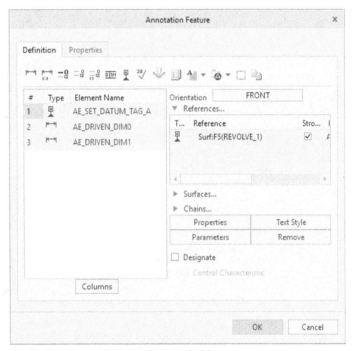 (TOP).

3. In the Model Tree, expand the **Footer**.

4. Select **D5_Datums** and click (Edit Definition) in the mini toolbar.

5. This opens the Annotation Feature dialog box shown in Figure 4–76.

Figure 4–76

6. In the Annotation Feature dialog box, click (Geometric Tolerance).

7. Select the surface shown in Figure 4–77.

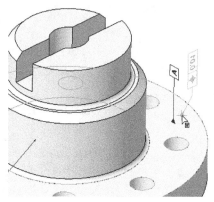

Figure 4–77

8. Press the middle mouse button in the location shown in Figure 4–78 to place the gtol.

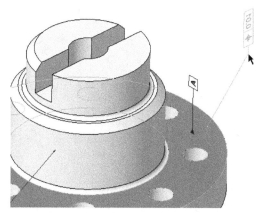

Figure 4–78

9. In the geometric *Tolerance* tab in the ribbon, expand **Geometric Characteristic** and select ▱ (Flatness).

10. In the Tolerances & Datum group, edit the tolerance to **0.1**.

11. Click on the screen to complete the gtol and the model updates as shown in Figure 4–79.

The gtol is clearly not oriented correctly, but you will remedy that in the next few steps.

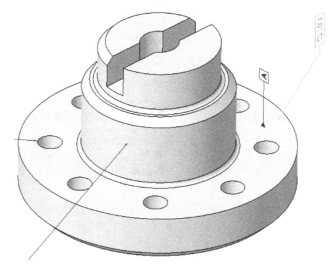

Figure 4–79

12. In the Annotation Feature dialog box, click **OK**.

13. Select the **D5_Datums** combination state.

14. Select the gtol, right-click, and select **Change Orientation**. The Annotation Plane dialog box opens as shown in Figure 4–80.

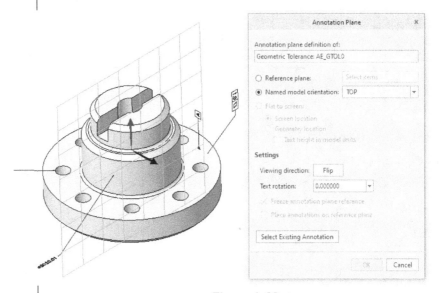

Figure 4–80

15. In the ANNOTATION PLANE dialog box, click **Flip**.

16. Enter **90** for the *Text Orientation*.

17. In the ANNOTATION PLANE dialog box, click **OK**.

18. Select the Datum Feature Symbol A and select ⚯ (Change Reference).

19. Select the gtol you just added and press the middle mouse button to place the Datum Feature Symbol in the position shown in Figure 4–81.

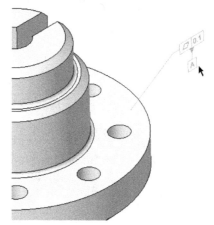

Figure 4–81

20. Select the **D5_Datums** combination state to reset the view, as shown in Figure 4–82.

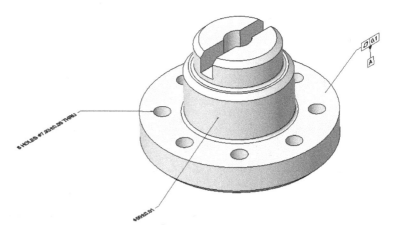

Figure 4–82

Task 3 - Create several more gtols.

1. In the **Footer**, select **D5_Datums** and click (Edit Definition) in the mini toolbar.

2. Select the (RIGHT) annotation plane.

3. In the Annotation Feature dialog box, click (Geometric Tolerance).

4. Select the dimension shown in Figure 4–83.

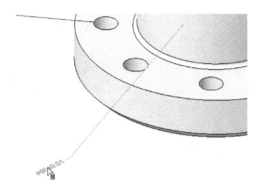

Figure 4–83

5. In the ribbon, expand **Geometric Characteristic** and select ⊥ (Perpendicularity).

6. In the primary datum field, type the letter **a**. Note that a is underlined in red. Click in the field again, and the symantic check indicates that it is an improper datum reference, as shown in Figure 4–84.

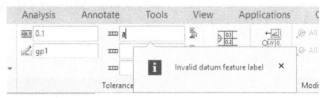

Figure 4–84

7. Edit the datum name to **A** and press <Enter>. Note that the datum reference turns green, indicating that the Datum Feature Symbol exists in the model.

8. Click on the screen to complete the gtol.

9. Press <Ctrl> and select both sides of the cylindrical surface as the gtol references.

10. In the Annotation Feature dialog box, click ⚚ (Datum Feature Symbol).

11. Select the gtol you just created and press the middle mouse button to place the Datum Feature Symbol, as shown in Figure 4–85.

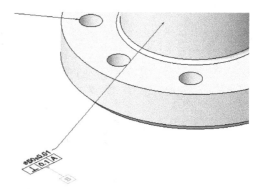

Figure 4–85

12. Select on the screen to complete the placement.

13. Select both sides of the cylindrical surface.

14. Click ▣▥ (Geometric Tolerance).

15. Select the dimension shown in Figure 4–86.

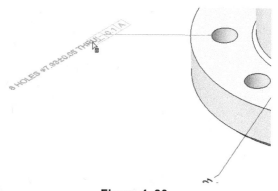

Figure 4–86

16. In the ribbon, expand **Geometric Characteristic** and select ⊕ (Position).

17. In the *Tolerance* field, ensure the tolerance value is **0.1**, then click to the left of **0.1**, as shown in Figure 4–87.

Figure 4–87

18. In the Symbols group, click ⌀⊤ (Symbols) and select ⌀ .

19. In the *Tolerance* field, click to the right of **0.1**, as shown in Figure 4–88.

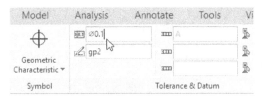

Figure 4–88

20. In the Symbols group, click ⌀⊤ (Symbols) and select Ⓜ .

21. In the *Secondary Reference* field, enter **B**.

22. Click on the screen to complete the gtol, which updates as shown in Figure 4–89.

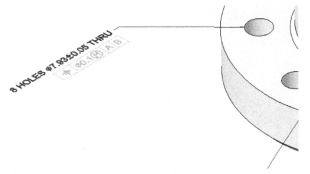

Figure 4–89

23. Select the surfaces of the holes. Remember that Creo
    Parametric treats a cylindrical surface as two halves. Ensure
    that you press and hold <Ctrl> and select both sides of each
    hole surface.

24. Click ⚏ (Datum Feature Symbol).

25. Select the gtol you just created and press the middle mouse
    button to place the Datum Feature Symbol as shown in
    Figure 4–90.

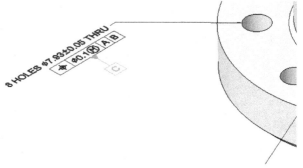

Figure 4–90

26. Select the surface references.

27. In the Annotation Feature dialog box, click **OK**.

28. Select the *D5_Datums* combination state tab to clean up
    the display. The completed combination state displays as
    shown in Figure 4–91.

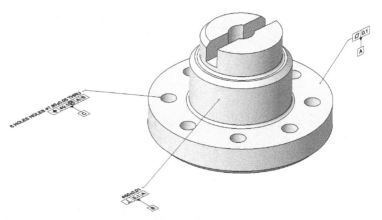

Figure 4–91

Task 4 - Create the D7_Gtols combination state.

1. In the In-graphics toolbar, click (View Manager).
2. Select the *All* tab.
3. Click **New**.
4. When prompted, enter **D7_Gtols** for the new combination state name and press <Enter>.
5. Click **Reference Originals**.
6. Double-click **D7_Gtols** to activate it.
7. Reorient the model approximately as shown in Figure 4–92.

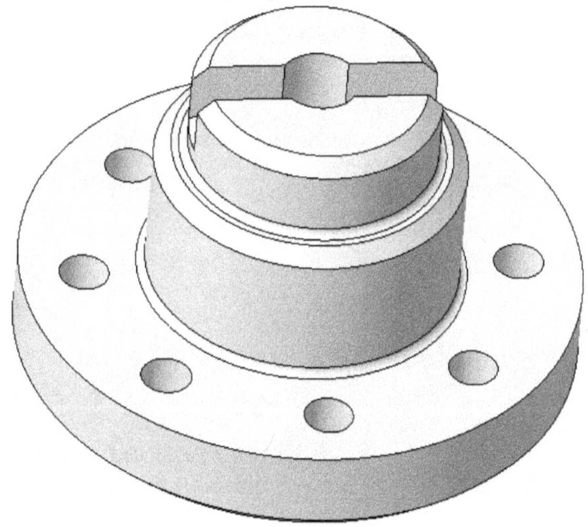

Figure 4–92

8. Select the *Orient* tab and click **New**.

9. Enter **D7_Gtols** as the name and press <Enter>.

10. Select the *All* tab.

11. Right-click on **D7_Gtols** and select **Redefine**.

12. Select **D7_Gtols** from the Orientation drop-down list.

13. In the D7_GTOLS dialog box, click **OK**.

14. Close the View Manager.

15. Select the **D5_Datums** combination state.

16. In the Detail Tree, select all of the annotations.

17. Select ⁺⁺ (Add to State) from the mini toolbar, as shown in Figure 4–93.

Figure 4–93

18. In the Assign Annotations dialog box, select D7_GTOLS, as shown in Figure 4–94.

Figure 4–94

19. Click **OK**.

20. Select the **D7_Gtols** combination state. The model displays as shown in Figure 4–95.

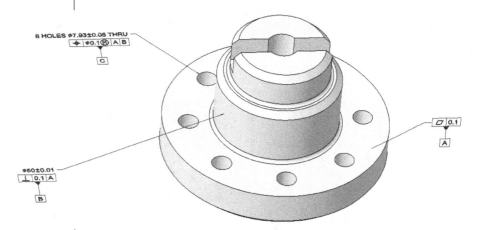

Figure 4–95

21. Drag the **D7_Gtols** combination state tab to between *D5_Datums* and *D8_Section_A*, as shown in Figure 4–96.

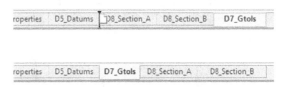

Figure 4–96

Task 5 - (Optional) Create additional geometric tolerances with limited instruction.

---

1. In the Annotation Features group in the ribbon, click ⬄ (Annotation Feature).

2. Create the dimension and geometric tolerance shown in Figure 4–97, using the steps in Task 2. Use Annotation Plane 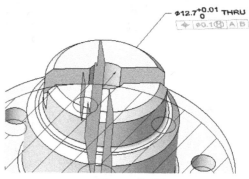 (RIGHT).

*Remember to **Flip** the dimension arrow and select the surface references.*

Figure 4–97

3. Create the dimension and geometric tolerance shown in Figure 4–98.

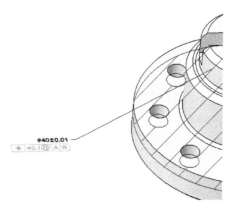

Figure 4–98

4. Create the dimension and geometric tolerance shown in Figure 4–99.

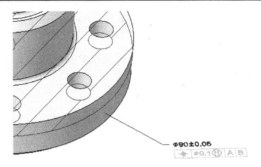

Figure 4–99

5. In the Annotation Feature dialog box, select the *Properties* tab and change the name to **D7_Gtols**.

6. Click **OK** in the Annotation Feature dialog box.

7. Select the *D7_Gtols* combination state tab.

8. In the Model Tree, right-click the **D7_GTOLS** annotation and select **Move to footer**.

9. Use **Move to Plane** for the center hole dimension to move it to the top surface.

10. Move the annotations as required to clean up the display as shown in Figure 4–100.

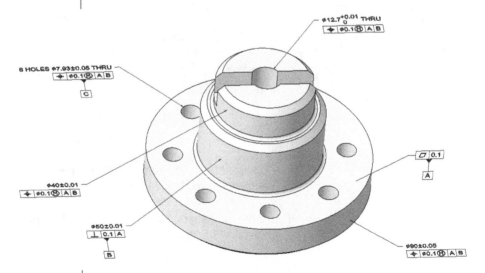

Figure 4–100

Task 6 - Investigate the Semantic Query tool.

1. In the *Annotate* tab of the ribbon, click  (Semantic Query).

2. The Semantic Query tool displays as shown in Figure 4–101.

Figure 4–101

3. Select the Datum Feature Symbol A on the screen.

4. In the Semantic Query dialog box, enable ⬜ (Primary References) and ⬜ (Secondary References), and the model displays as shown in Figure 4–102.

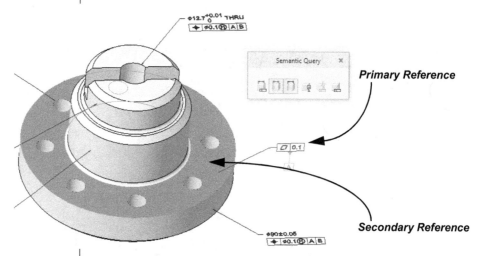

Figure 4–102

5. Click enabled ⬜ (Primary References) and ⬜ (Secondary References) to disable them.

6. Enable 🔲 (Associated GTOLs) and the model updates as shown in Figure 4–103.

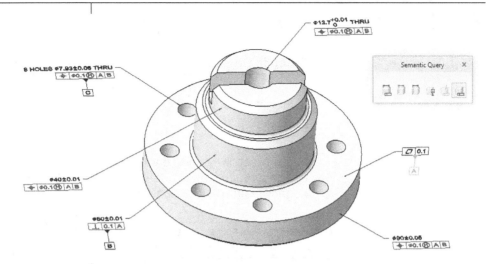

Figure 4–103

- The Semantic Query tool provides a quick way to visually investigate the semantic references within you models.

7. Select the *D0_Default* combination state tab.

8. Save the model and erase it from display.

Practice 4c

Handling Legacy Datums

Practice Objectives

- Open a part created in a previous release of Creo Parametric.
- Investigate the legacy datums using the Legacy Datum Annotation Conversion tool.
- Update legacy datums to Datum Feature Symbols.

In this practice, you will open a part started in an older release of Creo Parametric and update the legacy set datums using the Legacy Datum Annotation Conversion tool.

Task 1 - Use the Legacy Datum Annotation Conversion tool to update the datums.

1. Open **practice_4c.prt**.

2. A warning temporarily displays, indicating there are legacy annotations, as shown in Figure 4–104.

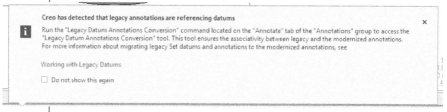

Creo has detected that legacy annotations are referencing datums

Run the "Legacy Datum Annotations Conversion" command located on the "Annotate" tab of the "Annotations" group to access the "Legacy Datum Annotations Conversion" tool. This tool ensures the associativity between legacy and the modernized annotations. For more information about migrating legacy Set datums and annotations to the modernized annotations, see

Working with Legacy Datums

☐ Do not show this again

Figure 4–104

3. Expand the **Annotation** node in the Model Tree.

4. Note the icons next to **gp0** and **gp1**, as shown in Figure 4–105.

The icon next to gp0 indicates a missing reference and the icon next to gp1 indicates a legacy annotation.

Figure 4–105

5. Select either geometric tolerance in the Model Tree, right-click, and select **Convert All**, as shown in Figure 4–106.

Figure 4–106

6. Click **Close** in the Conversion Warning dialog box, as shown in Figure 4–107.

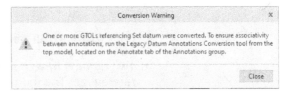

Figure 4–107

7. Select the *Annotate* tab.

8. Click **Annotations>Legacy Datum Annotation Conversion** to open the Legacy Datum Annotation Conversion tool, as shown in Figure 4–108.

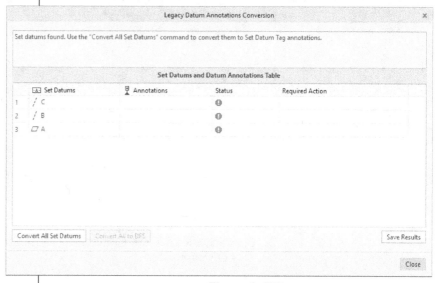

Figure 4–108

9. Click **Convert All Set Datums**.

10. Two datums have been converted, but require updated references. The third cannot be converted and requires that a Datum Feature Symbol be created, as shown in Figure 4–109.

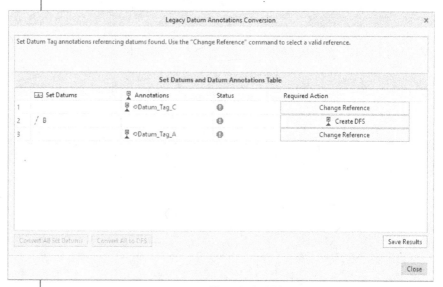

Figure 4–109

11. Place your cursor over each ⓘ icon in the status column to see a description of the issues, as shown in Figure 4–110.

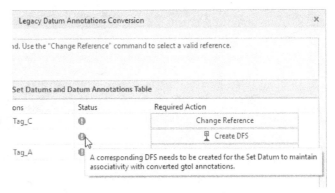

Figure 4–110

12. Click **Create DFS** for datum Set Datum B.

13. Select the **49.00** diameter dimension.

14. Middle-click to place the dimension as shown in Figure 4–111.

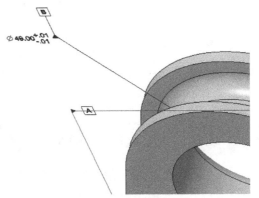

Figure 4–111

15. Note that **Datum_Tag_B** is added to the Annotations column and is displayed in green, as shown in Figure 4–112.

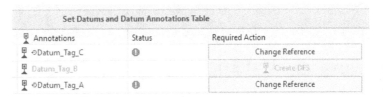

Figure 4–112

16. Click **Change Reference** for Datum_Tag_C.

17. Select the surface shown in Figure 4–113.

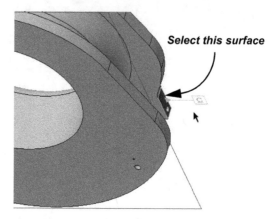

Select this surface

Figure 4–113

18. Middle-click to place the Datum Feature Symbol.

19. Note that **Datum_Tag_C** turns green in the Annotations column, and the Status and Required Action columns clear, as shown in Figure 4–114.

Figure 4–114

20. Click **Change Reference** for Datum_Tag_A.

21. In the *Annotate* tab, select  (RIGHT) for the annotation plane.

22. Select the surface shown in Figure 4–115.

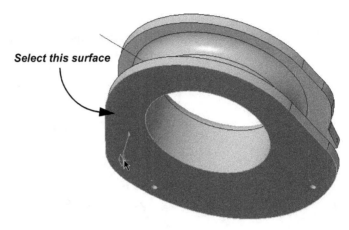

Figure 4–115

23. Middle-click to place the Datum Feature Symbol, as shown in Figure 4–116.

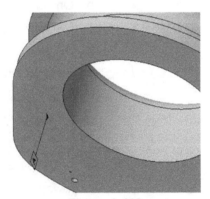

Figure 4–116

24. **Datum_Tag_A** turns green in the Annotations column, and the Status and Required Action columns clear.

25. Click **Close** in the Legacy Datum Annotation Conversion dialog box. The part would now be ready to continue working on it.

26. Close the part and erase it.

Chapter Review Questions

1. To annotate a model, you can show existing model dimensions or create new ones.

   a. True

   b. False

2. When you show existing model dimensions, they will display _____.

   a. On the Active Annotation Plane.

   b. As they were created originally in the model.

   c. You cannot show existing model dimensions.

3. Which of the following attachment types are permitted when creating dimensions?

   a. On Entity

   b. On Surface

   c. Midpoint

   d. Tangent

   e. All of the above

4. A Basic dimension is:

   a. An integer dimension.

   b. A dimension with a tolerance value.

   c. A theoretically exact value.

   d. Always a linear dimension.

5. Which of the following is not an available Geometric Tolerance type?

   a. ⊕

   b. ╱

   c. ⊥

   d. ⌀

Answers: 1.a, 2.b, 3.d, 4.c, 5.d

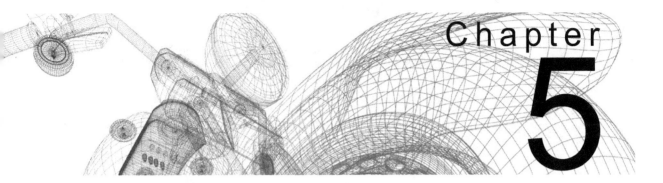

Additional Annotations

This chapter covers additional annotations such as notes, surface finish symbols, and other symbols.

Learning Objectives in This Chapter

- Create note annotations.
- Learn how to parametrically display hole notes.
- Edit note text.
- Create and place symbols.
- Understand the symbol palette.

5.1 Notes

Notes can be added to 3D models to communicate additional information about the model. You can create notes with or without leaders, and should create notes within an annotation feature.

The text in either case is defined on an annotation plane, so the orientation of the text is based on the orientation of the annotation plane you select, as shown in Figure 5–1. It is important that, as with other annotations, you only place notes in the planar orientation associated with the combination state to which they apply.

STATE: PRELIMINARY

DESTRUCTION NOTICE
DESTROY BY ANY METHOD THAT WILL PREVENT DISCLOSURE
OF CONTENTS OR RECONSTRUCTION OF THE DOCUMENT

DISTRIBUTION: C
DISTRIBUTION AUTHORIZED TO U.S. GOVERNMENT AGENCIES ONLY AND THEIR CONTRACTORS

WARNING
THIS DOCUMENT CONTAINS TECHNICAL DATA WHOSE EXPORT IS RESTRICTED

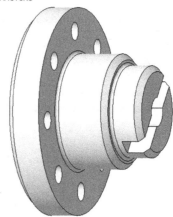

Figure 5–1

Select or create the required annotation plane from the Annotation Planes group in the ribbon. The orientation of the selected annotation plane defines the orientation of the text.

In the Annotation Features group of the ribbon, click

(Annotation Feature) or edit the definition of an existing annotation feature to open the Annotation Feature dialog box, as shown in Figure 5–2.

Figure 5–2

Select the appropriate note icon, based on the attachment type. The following options are available:

- (Unattached Note): Free placement in the annotation plane.

- (On Item Note): Attach note to another entity.

- (Tangent Leader Note): Attach note with a tangent leader.

- (Normal Leader Note): Attach note with a normal leader.

- (Leader Note): Attach note with a standard leader.

Click the middle mouse button to select the location for the note. The Format dashboard opens as shown in Figure 5–3.

Figure 5–3

Note that Annotation Features can contain multiple annotation elements, so you may have annotation features containing notes, dimensions, GTOLS, etc.

The text can be added by typing into the text field that displays in the location you selected. Alternatively, you can click  (Note From File) from the Text group, to import a text file.

The **config.pro** option *pro_note_dir* is used to point to the note library, where standard notes are stored. Using this option points directly to the defined directory when the (Note From File) option is used.

Regardless of the option, the text displays in the *Text* area of the Note dialog box, as shown in Figure 5–4.

ALL FILLETS
MUST BE REMOVED
FOR FEA ANALYSIS

Figure 5–4

Symbols can also be added into notes by selecting symbols from the palette shown in Figure 5–5.

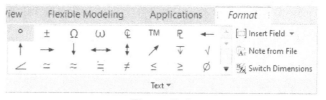

Figure 5–5

Parameters can also be added into notes, by typing an ampersand (&) before the parameter name. For example, if you had a parameter called MATERIAL, you could display its value in a note by typing **&MATERIAL**. Should the parameter update, the note will automatically update.

Several standard parameters are also available by clicking the ▭ (Insert Field) option in the Text group, as shown in Figure 5–6.

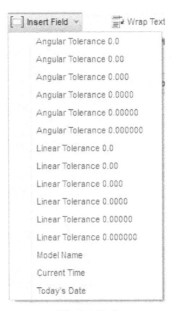

Figure 5–6

5.2 Displaying Hole Notes Parametrically

If you simply type in a note to describe a hole, it will not automatically update with changes to the model.

To ensure your notes update with the model, the dimensions must be called out parametrically. Consider the note shown in Figure 5–7.

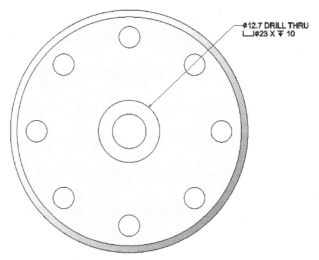

Figure 5–7

You could type in the values for the hole diameter and depth, and counterbore diameter and depth but if the hole dimensions were to change, the note would be out of sync with the model.

Therefore, before creating the note, select the hole to display its dimensions, then select the *Tools* tab and click 🔁 (Switch Dimensions). This displays the dimensions in parametric form, as shown in Figure 5–8.

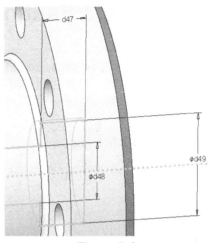

Figure 5–8

Make note of the dimension parameters, then set the appropriate combination state and annotation plane. Create a new annotation feature, or edit the definition of an existing one.

To use the parametric form of a dimension, type an ampersand (&) before the dimension name, d91, d92, etc.

To create the note, click ✓ᴬ (Leader Note) and select the attachment entity. Click the middle mouse button to place the note, and type it in. The note previously shown would be entered as shown in Figure 5–9.

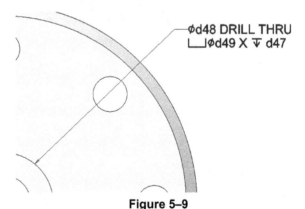

Figure 5–9

The counterbore and depth symbols are selected from the symbol palette in the ribbon.

Upon completion of the note, ensure that you select all of the surfaces to which it applies before completing the annotation feature.

5.3 Section Callouts

You have seen how to create sections in a previous chapter. Some organizations will also create callouts to those sections in other views. To do so, you must create a datum point on the section plane so that you can attach the leader of the callout.

In the ribbon, click **Point** in the **Datums** group menu, as shown in Figure 5–10.

Figure 5–10

Select the appropriate section plane and references to locate the point. In the combination state where you want to show the section callout, create a new annotation feature or edit the definition of an existing one, and create a note using the

$\mathcal{L}^{A}$ (Normal Leader Note) option.

Select the appropriate datum point, click the middle mouse button to place the note, and type **SECTION X**, where X is the letter for the section view. The next section, *Editing Text* shows an example for a callout to Section A, as shown in Figure 5–11.

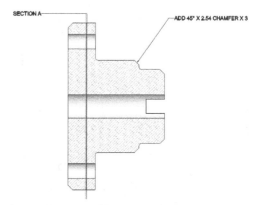

Figure 5–11

This method requires the use of Layer States to control datum display.

5.4 Editing Text

Editing Text Style

The text format can be edited using the Style group in the *Format* tab in the ribbon, as shown in Figure 5–12.

Figure 5–12

Here, you can change display settings for the note's text, including height and width, text orientation. color, and so on.

Editing Text Position

Once a note is placed, you can change the placement by selecting the Note in the list of annotation elements, then selecting **Properties** in the Annotation Feature dialog box. Drag the note to a different location on the screen.

Hyperlinks

You can turn notes into hyperlinks by clicking **Style>** 🔗 (Hyperlink) in the ribbon, or by right-clicking and selecting **Add Link**. This opens the Edit Hyperlink dialog box, as shown in Figure 5–13.

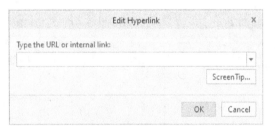

Figure 5–13

To open the hyperlink in the embedded browser, press <Ctrl> and select the link.

This can be very useful for linking to external documents or websites. For example, if you have a stock fastener in an assembly you could call it out in a note with a link to the website for the catalog from which it was obtained. This functionality is not supported in 3D PDF at this time.

5.5 Creating Symbols

Specific feature-based symbols (e.g., weld symbols or surface finish symbols) can be used to annotated your models. Figure 5–14 shows some examples of symbols that can be created and used. A custom symbol consists of symbol geometry, text (if required), and its properties (e.g., placement type, instance height, and attributes).

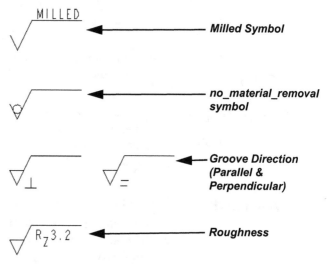

Milled Symbol

no_material_removal symbol

Groove Direction (Parallel & Perpendicular)

Roughness

Figure 5–14

A different symbol command might display on top. The last used icon is on top.

Select the *Annotate* tab. To create a new symbol, expand ⬡ (Symbol) and click ⬡ᴿ (Symbol Gallery) in the Annotations group in the *Annotate* tab, as shown in Figure 5–15.

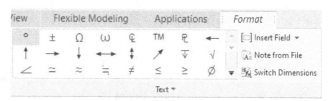

Figure 5–15

Select **Define** and enter a name for the symbol. The Symbol Edit window and menu opens, as shown in Figure 5–16.

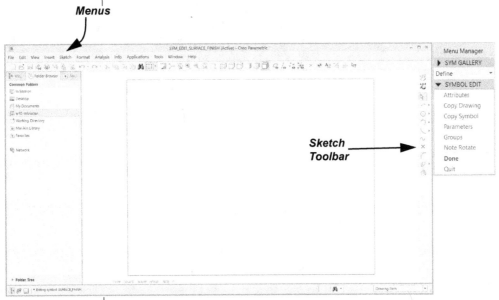

Figure 5–16

The symbol geometry consists of all of the 2D entities that are used in the symbol. For example, all of the entities in Figure 5–17 could be used to create a surface symbol.

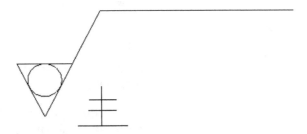

Figure 5–17

Use one of the following methods to create the 2D draft geometry that represents the symbol:

- Select **Copy Symbol** in the **SYMBOL EDIT** menu to copy existing symbols from the current symbol directory. The selected symbol is copied into the SYM_EDIT window.

- Select **Insert>Shared Data>From File** and select the file in the Open dialog box. The following file formats can be used: DXF, DWG, SET, CGM, IGES, STEP, etc.

- Click the icons in the Sketcher toolbar or use the options in the **Sketch** menu to sketch 2D geometry in the SYM_EDIT window.

You can create both fixed text and variable text in a symbol. Fixed text remains the same every time the symbol is used. Variable text enables you to either select from predefined text that was assigned when the symbol was created, or you can enter a new value when the symbol is placed. The symbol shown in Figure 5–18 has both fixed and variable text.

Figure 5–18

To use system and user-defined parameters in notes, you must enter the ampersand (&) symbol in front of the parameter.

To create text, select **Insert>Note** or click ![icon] in the toolbar. The note attributes for symbols are the same as those for creating drawing notes or 3D model annotations (e.g., leaders, text orientation, and justification). To add the note, select **Make Note** and enter the text in the message window.

To make text variable, you must use the following syntax when entering the note:

   \variable text

To complete note creation, select **Done/Return** in the **NOTE TYPES** menu.

The **Attributes** option in the **SYMBOL EDIT** menu enables you to define the requirements for placing the symbol.

Attributes must be defined to successfully create a symbol.

The *General* tab in the Symbol Definition Attributes dialog box is used to define the following attributes:

- Placement type and references

- Symbol instance height

- General attributes

The *General* tab in the Symbol Definition Attributes dialog box is shown in Figure 5–19.

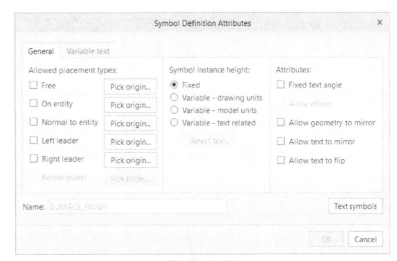

Figure 5–19

The **Allowed placement types** are described as follows:

Option	Description
Free	Enables the symbol to be placed without a leader.
On Entity	Enables the symbol to be placed on an entity.
Normal to Entity	Enables the symbol to be placed normal to an entity.
Left Leader	Enables the symbol to be placed with a leader to the left side of the symbol.
Right Leader	Enables the symbol to be placed with a leader to the right side of the symbol.
Radial Leader	Enables the symbol to be placed with a radial leader.

The **Symbol instance height** options are described as follows:

Option	Description
Fixed	Maintains the original symbol size.
Variable - Drawing Unit	Modifies the symbol size based on the drawing units.
Variable - Model Unit	Modifies the symbol size based on the model units.
Variable - Text Related	Modifies the symbol size based on the variable text used in the symbol.

The **Attributes** options are described as follows:

Option	Description
Fixed Text Angle	Maintains all text at the same angle.
Allow Elbow	Creates an elbow that is attached with a leader. If this attribute is not enabled during symbol creation you cannot move the text.
Allow geometry to mirror	Mirrors all geometry entities when you mirror the symbol instance.
Allow text to mirror	Mirrors all text entities when you mirror the symbol instance.
Allow text to flip	Flips all text entities when you rotate the symbol instance.

The *Var Text* tab is used to define the preset text values for each variable text entry. Each variable text entry has a different set of preset values. The *Var Text* tab in the Symbol Definition Attributes dialog box displays, as shown in Figure 5–20.

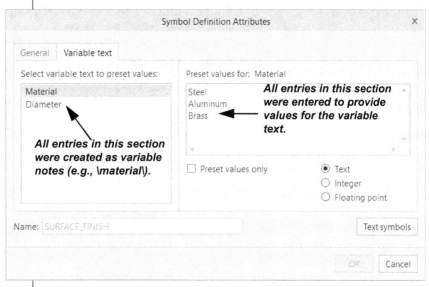

Figure 5–20

You can group the entities that create a symbol (e.g., 2D geometry and text) so that instances (or variations) of one generic symbol can be created. Groups can be created as **Independent** (default) or **Exclusive**. Independent groups can be displayed together in the same symbol, while exclusive groups cannot be displayed in the same symbol. The symbol and all of the geometry and text required are shown in the example on the left in Figure 5–21. Selected entities and text are selected to create groups, as shown in the example on the right in Figure 5–21.

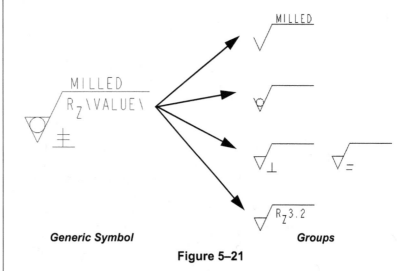

Generic Symbol   *Groups*

Figure 5–21

To create a group, select **Groups>Create**. The **SYM GROUPS** options are described as follows:

Option	Description
Create	Enables you to create a new group. Enter a name for the group and select the symbol entities to group.
Edit	Enables you to add or to remove entities from a selected group. For example, the menus shown below add or remove entities from group 2. 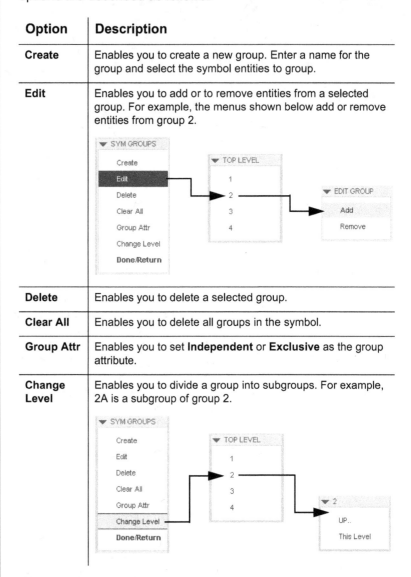
Delete	Enables you to delete a selected group.
Clear All	Enables you to delete all groups in the symbol.
Group Attr	Enables you to set **Independent** or **Exclusive** as the group attribute.
Change Level	Enables you to divide a group into subgroups. For example, 2A is a subgroup of group 2.

Select **Done** in the **SYMBOL EDIT** menu to complete the creation of the symbol. If you have not defined the attributes with regard to placing the symbol, you are prompted for this before you can complete it.

You can modify a symbol after it has been created using the options in the **SYM GALLERY** menu ( (Symbol Gallery)), as shown in Figure 5–22.

Figure 5–22

The options are described as follows:

Option	Description
Define	Enables you to define a user-defined symbol.
Redefine	Enables you to modify a user-defined symbol. The **GET SYMBOL** menu is shown below.

	Name	Redefines a symbol that has been retrieved.
	Pick Inst	Redefines a displayed symbol in the drawing.
	Retrieve	Retrieves a symbol for redefinition.
Delete		Enables you to delete all instances of a symbol.
Write		Enables you to save a symbol to disk.
Symbol Dir		Enables you to define the symbol directory.
Show Name		Enables you to display the name and path for a symbol in a drawing.

5.6 Placing a Custom Symbol

To place a symbol, select the *Annotate* tab to activate the annotation options.

Select the appropriate combination state and select the annotation plane from the Annotation Planes group in the ribbon. Create an annotation feature or, if one exists for the combination state, edit its definition.

Select or create the required annotation plane from the Annotation Planes group in the ribbon. The orientation of the selected annotation plane defines the orientation of the symbol.

To place a symbol in a model, expand ⚙ (Symbol) and click ⚙ (Custom Symbol) or right-click and select **Custom Symbol**. A symbol can also be placed as part of an Annotation Feature. The Custom Drawing Symbol dialog box displays, as shown in Figure 5–23.

Figure 5–23

Select the symbol in the **Symbol Name** menu or browse to select a symbol that is stored on the system. Only symbols that currently exist in the drawing are listed in the menu.

To define symbol placement, select an option in the **Type** drop-down menu in the *Placement* area in the *General* tab. The options vary depending on the placement type that was defined when the symbol was created. All of the available placement options are shown in Figure 5–24.

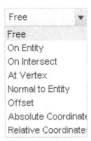

Figure 5–24

Once a placement option has been defined, drag the cursor onto the drawing and place the symbol using the left mouse button. The remaining two areas in the *General* tab enable you to define additional properties for the symbol. If available, you can customize the height, angle of display, and origin. The availability of these options is dependent on how the symbol was originally created.

The *Grouping* tab in the Custom Drawing Symbol dialog box is used to define the group that is placed in the drawing.
Figure 5–25 shows a *Grouping* tab for a symbol for which groups have been created. To define the symbol, you must select the groups that you want to include.

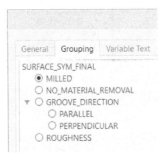

Figure 5–25

The *Variable Text* tab in the Custom Drawing Symbol dialog box is used to set the variable text values, as shown in Figure 5–26. If options are available for selection, they display in the Value drop-down list.

Figure 5–26

To complete symbol placement, click **OK** in the Drawing Symbol dialog box. This button is not available for selection until enough options have been defined to fully locate the symbol in the drawing.

5.7 Symbol Palette

The symbol palette enables you to display frequently used symbols in one location so that they can be easily added to a drawing. The symbol palette can be opened directly by expanding ⚠ (Symbol) and clicking ⚠ (Symbol from Palette) in the Annotations group in the *Annotate* tab or the Annotation Feature dialog box. Symbols can be selected in the palette and placed in the model. This increases your efficiency in creating and placing symbols.

*The **symbol_instance_palette_file** config.pro option can be defined with the path to the default symbol palette drawing file.*

Figure 5–27 shows the default Symbol Instance Palette, which displays generic symbols. The generic symbols can be placed using the free or on entity attachment types. The generic palette file is stored in the install location for Creo Parametric and is called **draw_symbol_palette.drw**. You can create custom palette files by creating drawing files and adding symbols to them. To switch between palettes, click **Open...** in the Symbol Instance Palette dialog box and select the file in the Open dialog box.

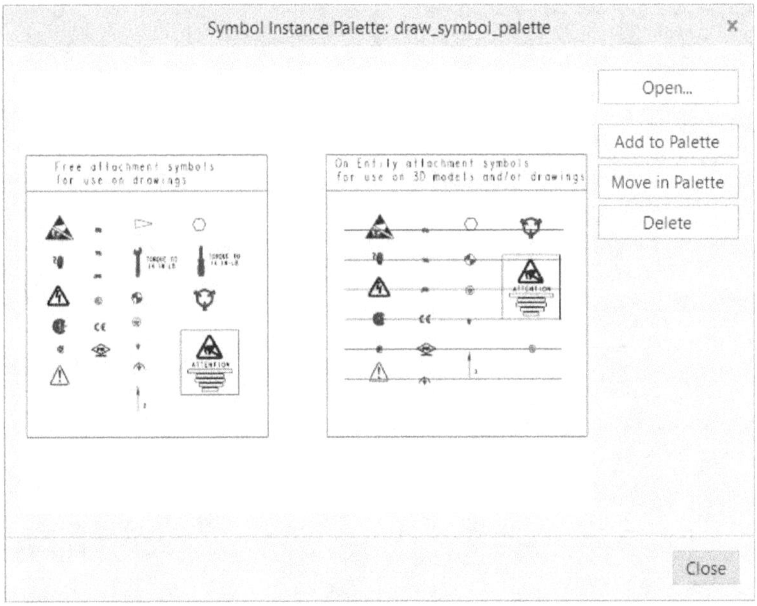

Figure 5–27

Symbols added to parts and assemblies can be displayed in a drawing using ⚠ in the Show Model Annotations dialog box.

5.8 Default Surface Finish Symbols

Select or create the required annotation plane from the Annotation Planes group in the ribbon. The orientation of the selected annotation plane defines the orientation of the symbol.

In the Annotation Features group of the ribbon click 7 (Annotation Feature) and click ³²√ (Surface Finish). Navigate to the appropriate folder and select the desired symbol. The Surface Finish dialog box opens, as shown in Figure 5–28.

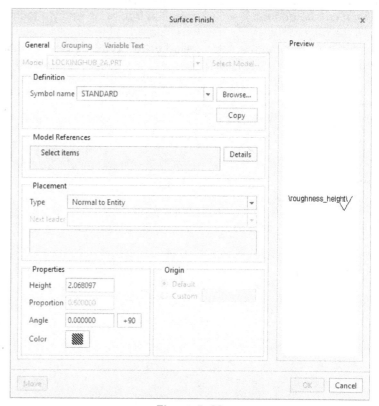

Figure 5–28

You can select the symbol from the Symbol name drop-down list.The default surface finish symbols are as follows:

Symbol Name	Symbol	Description
NO_VALUE		Basic surface texture symbol
STANDARD	1.6	Surface roughness (finished by any method)
STANDARD1	1.6	Surface roughness (material removal required)
STANDARD2	1.6	Surface Roughness (Material removal prohibited)

Click in the References reference collector if required, and select one or more surfaces on the model to which the symbol applies. To select multiple surfaces, press and hold <Ctrl> while selecting.

Select the leader type from the Placement Type drop-down list. The surface finish symbol can be placed **Normal to Entity**, **On Entity**, **Free** or **With Leaders**. Select one or more references for the leader. Additional properties such as **Height**, **Angle** and so on can also be edited.

To enter the roughness height, select the *Variable Text* tab. The roughness_height variable text is available for you to edit, as shown in Figure 5–29.

Figure 5–29

Click **OK** to complete the creation of the surface finish symbol. An example is shown in Figure 5–30.

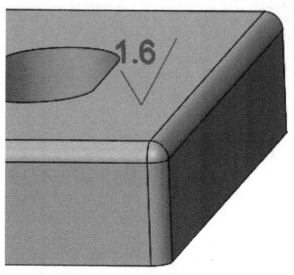

Figure 5–30

Practice 5a | Additional Annotations

Practice Objectives

- Add notes to a model.
- Add callouts to section planes.

In this practice, you will add notes to the model.

Task 1 - Open the part file.

1. If required, click ⬚ (Select Working Directory), navigate to the practice files folder and click **OK**.

2. Open **lockinghub_5a.prt**.

3. In the In-graphics toolbar, apply the following initial setup:

   - ⁺⁄⁎ *(Datum Display Filters):* All off

   - ⬚ *(Display Style):* ⬚ (Shading With Edges)

   - ⬚ *(Annotation Display):* Enabled

   - ⤙ *(Spin Center):* Disabled

Task 2 - Add a note for the D1_Site_Map combination state.

1. Select the *Annotate* tab if necessary.

2. Select the **D1_Site_Map** combination state tab.

3. In the Annotation Planes group in the ribbon, click ⬚ (FLAT TO SCREEN), if required.

4. In the Footer node of the Model Tree, select **D1_SITE_MAP** and select ⬚ (Edit Definition) in the mini toolbar.

5. Click ᴬ⬚ (Note) to create a note.

6. Select a screen location in the position shown in Figure 5–31.

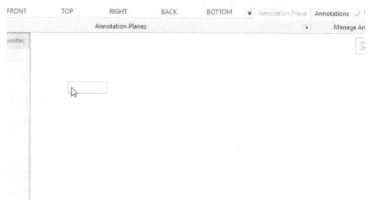

Figure 5–31

7. Type **SITE MAP** for the text and click on the screen to complete the text.

8. In the Annotation Feature dialog box, right-click on the note and select **Text Style**.

These options can be set in the ribbon as well, but at the time of writing this content, it is easier to use the Text Style dialog box.

9. Edit the *Height* to **8**.

10. Click the ▇ color swatch.

11. Click the ▇ color swatch and click **OK**.

12. In the Text Style dialog box, click **OK**.

13. In the Annotation Feature dialog box, click ⁴≣ (Note) to create another note.

14. Click on the screen in the approximate location shown in Figure 5–32.

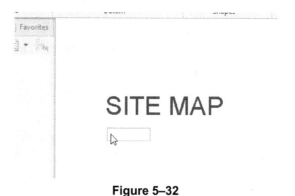

Figure 5–32

15. In the ribbon, click 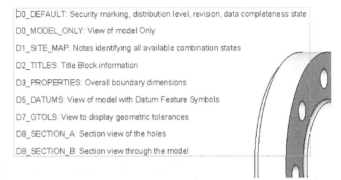 (Note From File).Double-click on **site_map.txt**.

16. The note updates as shown in Figure 5–33.

SITE MAP

D0_DEFAULT: Security marking, distribution level, revision, data completeness state

D0_MODEL_ONLY: View of model Only

D1_SITE_MAP: Notes identifying all available combination states

D2_TITLES: Title Block information

D3_PROPERTIES: Overall boundary dimensions

D5_DATUMS: View of model with Datum Feature Symbols

D7_GTOLS: View to display geometric tolerances

D8_SECTION_A: Section view of the holes

D8_SECTION_B: Section view through the model

Figure 5–33

17. Click on the screen to complete the note.

18. Right-click on the note in the Annotation Feature dialog box and select **Text Style**.

19. Edit the *Height* to **5**.

20. Click the ▪ color swatch.

21. Click the ▪ color swatch and click **OK**.

22. In the Text Style dialog box, click **OK**.

23. In the Annotation Feature dialog box, click **OK**. The **D1_Site_Map** state updates as shown in Figure 5–34.

SITE MAP

D0_DEFAULT: Security marking, distribution level, revision, data completeness state

D0_MODEL_ONLY: View of model Only

D1_SITE_MAP: Notes identifying all available combination states

D2_TITLES: Title Block information

D3_PROPERTIES: Overall boundary dimensions

D5_DATUMS: View of model with Datum Feature Symbols

D7_GTOLS: View to display geometric tolerances

D8_SECTION_A: Section view of the holes

D8_SECTION_B: Section view through the model

Figure 5–34

Task 3 - Add a note for the D8_Section_B combination state that uses a leader.

---

1. Select the *D8_Section_B* combination state.

2. Click (FRONT) to set the annotation plane.

3. Select the surface of the chamfer and click **d1** (Edit Dimensions), as shown in Figure 5–35.

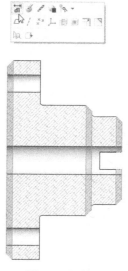

Figure 5–35

4. In the ribbon, select the *Tools* tab and click <img_1 inline/> (Switch Dimensions). The dimension displays symbolically as shown in Figure 5–36.

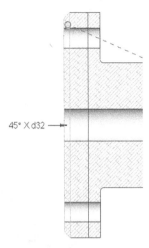

45° X d32

Figure 5–36

5. Note the symbolic dimension (d32) and click (Switch Dimensions) to return to standard dimension display.

6. Click on the screen to clear any selections, then select the *Annotate* tab.

7. In the ribbon in the Annotation feature group, click (Annotation Feature).

8. In the Annotation Feature dialog box, expand (Note) and select (Leader Note).

9. Select the surface of the chamfer and press the middle mouse button in the location shown in Figure 5–37 to place the note.

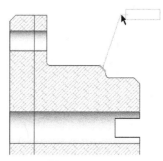

Figure 5–37

10. Type **ADD &d32 CHAMFER 3X**.

11. Click on the screen, and the note updates, as shown in Figure 5–38.

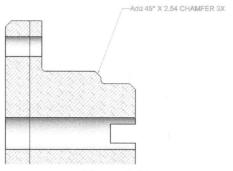

Add 45° X 2.54 CHAMFER 3X

Figure 5–38

12. In the *Properties* tab of the Annotation Feature dialog box, edit the name to **D8_Section_B**.

13. Click **OK** in the Annotation Feature dialog box.

14. Move **D8_SECTION_B** to the Regeneration footer.

Task 4 - Create a Layer State for when the Section A and Section B planes are displayed and a Layer State for when no plane is to be displayed.

---

1. In the In-graphics toolbar, click (View Manager).

2. Select the *Layers* tab.

3. Click **New** and edit the name to **D8_Section_A**.

4. Click **New** and edit the name to **D8_Section_B**.

5. Click **New** and edit the name to **No_Section**.

6. **No_Section** is the active Layer State, as shown in Figure 5–39.

Figure 5–39

7. In the Model Tree, click  (Show)>**Layer Tree**.

8. In the Layer Tree, right-click and select **New Layer**.

9. Edit the name to **D8_Section_A**.

10. Click (Show)>**Model Tree** and select the **SECTION_B** datum plane.

11. Click **OK** in the Layer Properties dialog box.

12. Click (Show)>**Layer Tree**.

13. In the Layer Tree, right-click and select **New Layer**.

14. Edit the name to **D8_Section_B**.

15. Click (Show)>**Model Tree** and select the **SECTION_A** datum plane.

16. Click **OK** in the Layer Properties dialog box.

17. Click (Show)>**Layer Tree**.

18. In the Layer Tree, right-click and select **New Layer**.

19. Edit the name to **No_Section**.

20. Click ☷ ▾ (Show)>**Model Tree**.

21. In the Layer Tree, select the **SECTION_A** and **SECTION_B** datum planes.

22. Click **OK**.

Task 5 - Set the display for the Layer States.

---

1. The **No_Section** Layer State is still active.

2. Click ☷ ▾ (Show)>**Layer Tree**.

This Layer State turns off the display of all datum planes.

3. Select the **01__PART_ALL_DTM_PLN, 01__PRT_DEF_DTM_PLN, D8_SECTION_A**, and **D8_SECTION_B** layers, right-click, and select **Hide**, as shown in Figure 5–40.

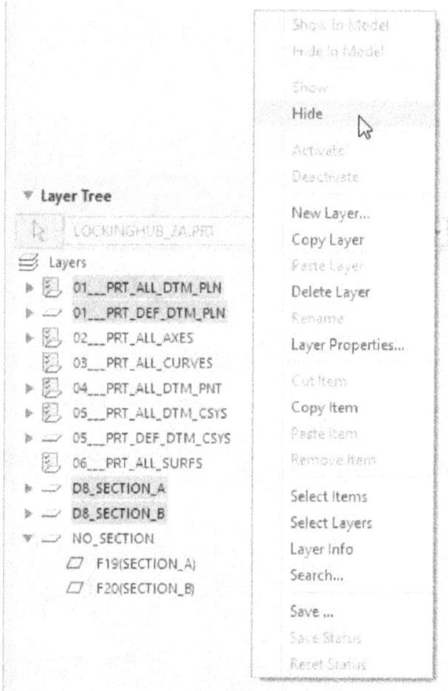

Figure 5–40

4. In the View Manager, click **Edit>Save**.

5. Click **OK** in the Save Display Elements dialog box.

6. In the View Manager, double-click **D8_Section_A** to activate it.

*This Layer State hides all datum planes except for the **SECTION_B** plane.*

7. Select the **01__PART_ALL_DTM_PLN, 01__PRT_DEF_DTM_PLN, D8_SECTION_B**, and **NO_SECTION** layers, right-click, and select **Hide**.

8. Expand the **D8_SECTION_A** layer, right-click **F19(SECTION_B)**, and select **Show**.

9. In the View Manager, click **Edit>Save**.

10. Click **OK** in the Save Display Elements dialog box.

11. In the View Manager, double-click **D8_Section_B** to activate it.

*This Layer State hides all datum planes except for the **SECTION_A** plane.*

12. Select the **01__PART_ALL_DTM_PLN, 01__PRT_DEF_DTM_PLN, D8_SECTION_A**, and **NO_SECTION** layers, right-click, and select **Hide**.

13. Expand the **D8_SECTION_B** layer, right-click **F19(SECTION_A)**, and select **Show**.

14. In the View Manager, click **Edit>Save**.

15. Click **OK** in the Save Display Elements dialog box.

16. Close the View Manager.

Task 6 - Apply the Layer States to the appropriate views.

1. Select the *D0_Default* combination state tab.

2. Right-click and select **Redefine**.

3. In the dialog box, select **No_Section** from the Layers drop-down list, as shown in Figure 5–41.

Figure 5–41

---

4. Click **OK**.

5. Repeat the previous steps for the *D0_Model_Only*, *D1_Site_Map*, *D2_Titles*, *D3_Properties*, *D5_Datums*, and *D7_Gtols* combination states.

6. Select the *D8_Section_A* combination state tab.

7. Right-click and select **Redefine**.

8. In the dialog box, select **D8_Section_A** from the Layers drop-down list.

9. Click **OK**.

10. Select the *D8_Section_B* combination state tab.

11. Right-click and select **Redefine**.

12. In the dialog box, select **D8_Section_B** from the Layers drop-down list.

13. Click **OK**.

Task 7 - Add a callout for SECTION B in the D8_Section_A combination state.

---

1. Select the *D8_Section_A* combination state tab.

2. In the In-graphics toolbar, enable ⬚ (Plane Display).

3. In the Annotation Planes group, click ◀ (RIGHT), if required.

4. Expand the Datums drop-down list on the right-hand side of the ribbon and select ˣˣ (Point).

5. In the Model Tree, select datum plane **SECTION_B** as the reference plane.

6. Click in the *Offset references* field, press and hold <Ctrl>, and select datum **TOP** and **RIGHT** in the Model Tree. The Datum Point dialog box updates as shown in Figure 5–42.

Figure 5–42

7. Edit the *Offset* value from the **RIGHT** plane to **0** and the **TOP** plane to **50**. The Datum Point dialog box displays as shown in Figure 5–43.

Note that your offset planes may be in the reverse order, depending on the order in which they were selected.

Figure 5–43

8. Click **OK** in the Datum Point dialog box.

9. In the Model Tree, expand the **Footer**, select the **D8_Section_A** annotation feature, and click 🖌 (Edit Definition) in the mini toolbar.

10. Expand the ᴬ≣ (Note) flyout and select ⌐ᴬ (Normal Leader Note).

11. In the Model Tree, select **PNT1**.

12. Click the middle mouse button approximately in the location shown in Figure 5–44.

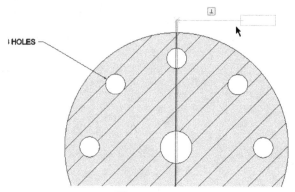

Figure 5–44

13. Type **SECTION B**, then click anywhere on the screen to complete the note.

14. Click **OK** in the Annotation Feature dialog box and the model updates as shown in Figure 5–45.

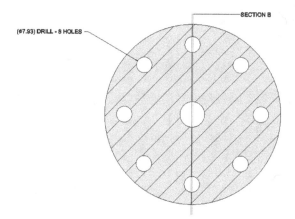

Figure 5–45

15. Select the **SECTION B** note, right-click on the end of the leader, and select **Arrow Style>Single Arrow**.

Task 8 - Add a callout for SECTION A in the D8_Section_B combination state.

---

1. Select the *D8_Section_B* combination state tab.

2. In the Annotation Planes group, click ⬚ (FRONT), if required.

3. Expand the Datums drop-down list in the ribbon and select
   ×× (Point).

4. Select datum plane **SECTION_A** as the reference plane.

5. Click in the *Offset references* field, press and hold <Ctrl>, and
   select datum **TOP** and **FRONT** in the Model Tree.

6. Edit the *Offset* value from the **FRONT** plane to **0** and the **TOP**
   plane to **50**. The Datum Point dialog box displays as shown in
   Figure 5–46.

*Note that your offset
planes may be in the
reverse order,
depending on the order
in which they were
selected.*

Figure 5–46

7. Click **OK** in the Datum Point dialog box.

8. In the Model Tree, expand the **Footer**, select the
   D8_Section_B annotation feature, and click ✎ (Edit
   Definition) in the mini toolbar.

9. Expand the ᴬ≣ (Note) flyout and select ⌐ᴬ (Normal Leader
   Note).

10. In the Model Tree, select **PNT1**.

11. Click the middle mouse button approximately in the location shown in Figure 5–47.

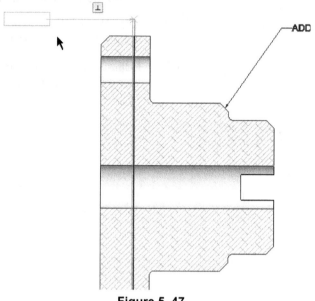

Figure 5–47

12. Type **SECTION A**, then click anywhere on the screen to complete the note.

13. Click **OK** in the Annotation Feature dialog box and the model updates as shown in Figure 5–48.

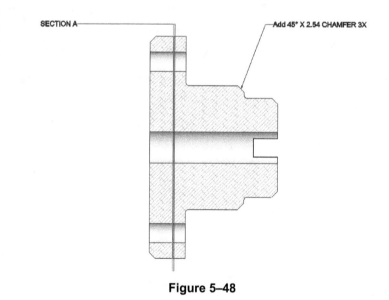

Figure 5–48

14. Select the **SECTION A** note, right-click on the end of the leader, and select **Arrow Style>Single Arrow**.

15. Switch between combination states to review the model. Note that the datum plane features only show in the **D8_Section_A** and **D8_Section_B** combination states.

16. Select the **D0_Default** combination state.

17. Save and erase the model.

Practice 5b

Custom Symbols

Practice Objectives

- Create a new symbol.
- Place the newly created symbol on the model.
- Place a surface finish symbol on the model using the Normal option.

In this practice, you will create a symbol that contains a logo and text that pulls parameters from the model, as shown in Figure 5–49.

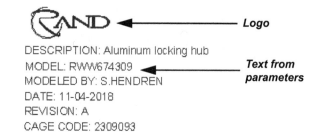

DESCRIPTION: Aluminum locking hub
MODEL: RWW674309
MODELED BY: S.HENDREN
DATE: 11-04-2018
REVISION: A
CAGE CODE: 2309093

Figure 5–49

Task 1 - Open a part file.

1. If required, click ⌖ (Select Working Directory), navigate to the practice files folder, and click **OK**.

2. Open **lockinghub_5b.prt**.

3. In the In-graphics toolbar, apply the following initial setup:

   - ⁂ *(Datum Display Filters):* All off

   - ▱ *(Display Style):* ▱ (Shading With Edges)

   - ▱ *(Annotation Display):* Enabled

   - ⁂ *(Spin Center):* Disabled

Task 2 - Create a symbol.

1. Select the *Annotate* tab.

A different symbol command might display on top. The last used icon is on top.

2. Expand ⚬ (Symbol) and select ⚬ᴿ (Symbol Gallery), as shown in Figure 5–50.

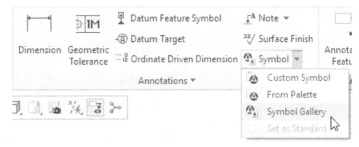

Figure 5–50

3. In the **SYM GALLERY** menu, select **Define**.

4. Enter **title_block** as the name of the symbol. The SYM_EDIT_SURFACE_SYMBOL window displays, where you can sketch the symbol, and the **SYMBOL EDIT** menu displays as shown in Figure 5–51.

Figure 5–51

*The **Copy Symbol** option copies symbols from a directory.*

5. In the **SYMBOL EDIT** menu, select **Copy Symbol**.

6. In the Open dialog box, click **Working Directory** if required, and double-click on **logo.sym**.

7. Click on the screen to place the note, then press the middle mouse button to complete the placement.

8. Enter **1** when prompted for the instance height. The logo displays as shown in Figure 5–52.

Figure 5–52

9. Click **Done**.

10. Note that the top menu bar displays as grayed out until you make a selection. In the top menu bar, select **View>Draft Grid** at the top of the main window. The **GRID MODIFY** menu displays.

11. Select **Show Grid**.

12. Select **Grid Params>X&Y Spacing** to change the spacing of the grid lines to **1**.

13. In the **CART PARAMS** menu, select **Done/Return**.

14. In the toolbar, click ᴬ☰ (Note).

15. Accept the defaults and select **Make Note** in the **NOTE TYPES** menu.

16. Select the location for the note, as shown in Figure 5–53.

Place the note here

DESCRIPTION: \&description\
Figure 5–53

17. Enter **DESCRIPTION: \&description** in the message window, press <Enter>.

18. Enter **MODEL: \&model_number** in the message window, press <Enter>.

19. Enter **MODELED BY: \\&modeled_by** in the message window, press <Enter>.

20. Enter **DATE: \\&modeled_date** in the message window, press <Enter>.

21. Enter **REVISION: \\&rev** in the message window, press <Enter>.

22. Enter **CAGE_CODE: \\&cage_code** in the message window, press <Enter> twice, and select **Done/Return**.

23. If required, modify the text height. Right-click on the text and select **Properties**. Select the *Text Style* tab and change the text height to **0.20** using the *Height* field.

24. In the **SYMBOL EDIT** menu, select **Done**.

25. In the Symbol Definition Attributes dialog box, enable the **Free** placement option.

26. Select just above the R in Rand as the placement origin.

27. Enable the **Variable - model units** option.

28. Click **OK**.

29. In the **SYM EDIT** menu, select **Done**.

30. In the **SYM GALLERY** menu, select **Write>Name> TITLE_BLOCK** and press <Enter> to save it to the Working Directory.

31. In the **SYM GALLERY** menu, select **Done**.

Task 3 - Add the title block symbol to the D2_Titles combination state.

---

1. Select the *D2_Titles* combination state tab.

2. Click ⌣ (FLAT TO SCREEN).

3. In the Footer section of the Model Tree, select **D2_Titles** and click ⌁ (Edit Definition) in the mini toolbar.

4. Click ⌀ (Custom Symbol).

5. Click ⌂ (Working Directory) in the *Common Folders* area in the Open dialog box.

6. Double-click on **title_block.sym**.

7. Click in the location shown in Figure 5–54 to place the symbol.

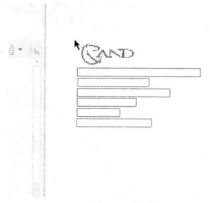

Figure 5–54

8. Click **OK** in the Symbol dialog box and click **OK** in the Annotation Feature dialog box.

9. Click on the *D2_Titles* combination state tab to clean up the display, and the combination state displays as shown in Figure 5–55.

The symbol extracts parameters from the model and displays them.

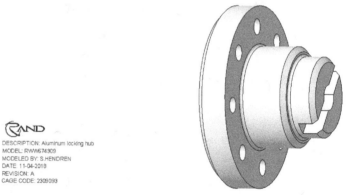

DESCRIPTION: Aluminum locking hub
MODEL: RWW674309
MODELED BY: S.HENDREN
DATE: 11-04-2018
REVISION: A
CAGE CODE: 2309093

Figure 5–55

10. Move the **D2_Titles** annotation feature to the Regeneration footer.

Task 4 - Add a surface finish symbol to the D7_Gtols combination state.

1. Select the *D7_Gtols* combination state tab.

2. Select the **D7_Gtols** annotation feature in the Footer node in Model Tree and click (Edit Definition) in the mini toolbar.

3. Select the (TOP) annotation plane.

4. Click (Surface Finish).

5. Click **Browse**.

6. Double-click on the *machined* folder and double-click on **standard1.sym**.

7. Select the *Variable Text* tab and set the *roughness_height* to **16**.

8. Select the *General* tab.

9. Select the surface shown in Figure 5–56.

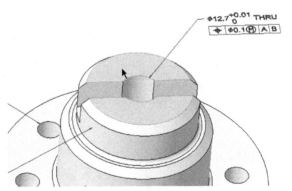

Figure 5–56

10. Select **Normal to Entity** from the Placement Type drop-down list.

11. Select the location shown in Figure 5–57.

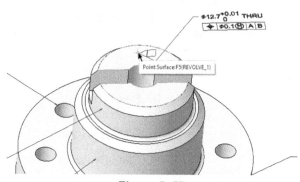

Figure 5–57

12. Edit the *Height* to **3.0** and change the color to [ ].

13. Press the middle mouse button to complete the annotation placement and click **OK** in the Surface Finish dialog box.

14. Click **OK** in the Annotation Feature dialog box. The symbol displays, as shown in Figure 5–58.

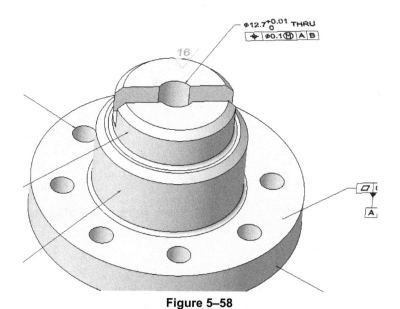

Figure 5–58

15. Select the **D0_Default** combination state.

16. Save the model and close it.

Chapter Review Questions

1. In a symbol, the fixed text remains the same every time the symbol is used.

   a. True

   b. False

2. Variable text enables you to select from predefined text that was assigned when the symbol was created. You cannot enter a new value when the symbol is placed.

   a. True

   b. False

3. What is the advantage of using a symbol palette?

   a. Group frequently used symbols together.

   b. Enables you to place multiple symbols at the same time.

   c. Enables you to change the symbols.

   d. Enables you to set the variable text.

4. When creating a note Flat to Screen, which of the following can be used for placement?

   a. Unattached Note

   b. On Item Note

   c. Normal Leader

   d. Tangent Leader

   e. Leader Note

5. Notes can be typed in or loaded from an existing file.

   a. True

   b. False

6. To include model parameter in a note or symbol, precede the parameter name with:

   a. @

   b. &

   c. %

   d. !

7. Surface finish symbols can be positioned parallel or normal to a surface.

    a. True

    b. False

Answers: 1.a, 2.b, 3.a, 4.a, 5.a, 6.b, 7.a